The Book Of Waters

The Book Of Waters

Text by Steven Schwartz
Designed by Gary Cosimini
Produced by Steven Heller
Photographs by Ed Spiro
Conceived by Sarah Jane Freymann

A & W Visual Library
New York

Acknowledgments

Thank you to Sarah Jane: wife, agent, thinker of the idea in the first place, French translator, and Spanish and Italian translator if she had to. Thank you also to Steve Heller, who not only produced this book, but is also a dear friend. And to Gary Cosimini, the designer. (We all wanted to call the book *On the Waterfront* and have a picture of Brando adorning the cover with a bottle of water superimposed in his hand. Clearer minds, however, prevailed.) Thank you to Ed Spiro, who was responsible for making all the original photographs (and could probably have found a way to bring off the Brando cover); and to John Scott, of Health Waters of New York, who was an invaluable source of information. And finally, thank you to all the water bottlers and distributors without whose cooperation this book would not have been possible.

Credits

Steven Guarnaccia: drawings on pages 15, 16, 27, 43, 73, 96
Bettmann Archive engravings on pages 2, 10, 12
Leslie Cabarga: cover typography

Published by
A & W Publishers, Inc.
95 Madison Avenue
New York, New York 10016

Library of Congress Cataloging in Publication Data

Schwartz, Steven, 1942–
  The book of waters.

  (A & W visual library)
  1. Mineral waters.   I. Title.
TN923.S35   641.3   78-65674
ISBN: 0-89104-140-0
ISBN: 0-89104-139-7 pbk.

Printed in the United States of America

For the presence of Sarah Jane and the memory

of my mother

Contents

Water, Water
Everywhere . . .
Page 13

Apollinaris
from Bad Neuenahr,
West Germany
Page 21

Badoit
from Saint Galmier,
France
Page 27

Bru
from Chevron,
Belgium
Page 29

Caddo Valley
from Caddo Valley,
Arkansas
Page 31

Contrexéville
from Contrexéville,
France
Page 33

Deer Park
from the Nestlé Company
Page 37

Ephrata Diamond
from Ephrata,
Pennsylvania
Page 39

Evian
from Evian-les-Bains,
France
Page 41

Fachingen
from Fachingen,
West Germany
Page 45

Fiuggi
from Fiuggi,
Italy
Page 47

Gerolsteiner Sprudel
from Gerolstein,
West Germany
Page 51

Mattoni
from Kysibel-Kyselka,
Czechoslovakia
Page 53

Mountain Valley
from Hot Springs,
Arkansas
Page 57

Perrier
from Vergeze,
France
Page 63

Poland Water
from Poland Springs,
Maine
Page 69

Ramlösa
from Helsingborg,
Sweden
Page 73

San Pellegrino
from Bergamo,
Italy
Page 77

Saratoga Vichy
from Saratoga Springs,
New York
Page 79

Spa Reine
from Liège,
Belgium
Page 83

Vichy Célestins
from Vichy,
France
Page 87

Vittel
from Vittel,
France
Page 93

Water begins innocently enough when atoms of hydrogen and oxygen combine. Then, without so much as a "please" or a "thank you," water falls from the sky as rain, forms streams, lakes, and seas, burbles up from the ground as springs, and winds up covering about 70 percent of the earth's surface. It also constitutes most of the living tissue in the human body, comprising 92 percent of blood plasma, 80 percent of muscle mass, 60 percent of red blood cells, and 50 percent of what's left.

Water then appears as a long, rather technical encyclopedia definition:

> Mineral water, spring water containing various mineral salts, especially the carbonates, chlorides, phosphates, silicates, sulphides, and sulphates of calcium, iron, lithium, potassium, sodium, and other metals. Various gases may also be present, for example, carbon dioxide, hydrogen sulphide, nitrogen, and inert gases.

And finally, water makes its way into bottles—from locales as diverse as France, Italy, Sweden, West Germany, Belgium, Czechoslovakia, and Arkansas, bearing such labels as Perrier, Fiuggi, Ramlösa, Apollinaris, Spa, Mattoni, and Mountain Valley.

A new industry is burgeoning under our very noses. Oil isn't our most precious liquid substance. Water is.

Water from the Fountain Tree *in the Canary Islands*

Water, Water Everywhere...

First things first. *All* water on God's green earth is mineral water. The instant a cloud becomes rain, water begins to acquire minerals from the air. After the rain hits the ground and begins to seep into the soil, it acquires even more minerals. And when underground springs journey upward toward the surface, the water is enriched by the layers of rock through which it passes.

In fact, it's the presence of minerals that accounts for a water's taste. The quantity and balance of the minerals yield either a pleasant flavor, or one that prompts a sense memory of mouths being washed out with soap.

Do not, however, confuse the term "mineral water" with "bottled water." There are over 700 brands of *bottled water* offered for sale in the United States, and annual consumption is in the 1.6 billion quart range. *But* only about 20 percent of that figure is what can be called "natural" water, or mineral water. The rest is tap water that has been processed, treated, or purified in some way.

Imported mineral water, by contrast, is bottled at its source in a pure, unadulterated state. And it is governed by strict regulations administered by each country's department of health.

Federal regulations in the United States do not require bottling at the source, and do not even require that the name of the source appear on the label. But no cheating is allowed. If the label of a domestic bottle says "natural spring water," then that's what it's supposed to be.

The most popular mineral waters sold in the United States didn't get that way by accident. Advertising and availability were certainly contributing factors. But the consistent quality of the product was most important.

All of the domestic and imported waters in this book share common characteristics. They have long, established histories and reputations. They come from sources that are rigidly guarded against urban wastes, pesticides, detergents, fallout, and added chemicals. They will always taste the same whenever or wherever they are drunk because the waters maintain a consistent temperature and mineral composition, and their source maintains a consistent year-round flow. Furthermore, the waters are bottled without being pumped to the surface of the earth, and the majority are bottled without having anything added to them that didn't arrive with them. And finally, most of the waters initially gained their reputations at a spa, where their therapeutic properties drew people in the first place.

Interestingly enough, the taste of the real thing cannot be duplicated in a laboratory. Minerals injected into water under test-tube conditions do not dissolve properly. Such a potion may be interesting to a scientist, but anyone else would have to have a powerful peanut-butter-sandwich-on-rye thirst to be satisfied.

After all is said and done, though, one can still stroll over to a convenient sink and turn on a tap. So why pay a premium price for a commodity that's so abundantly and cheaply provided? There seem to be many answers to this question, and safety is one of them.

For centuries, people in Europe have differentiated between the water they use to wash their clothes, clean their floors, and flush their toilets—and the water they drink, or sometimes sprinkle delicately on their faces. A major reason for this was that large bodies of their water used to be contaminated. The advice "Don't drink the water" was as indispensable for an American traveling abroad as was a passport or voltage converter. Bottled water from a well-known spring was the only safe bet.

But today in the United States, tap water can sometimes look like what's left in the washing machine after a load of sweatsocks has been done. And it doesn't taste much better, either.

So Americans are beginning to raise the question of water purity.

A United States Public Health Service study conducted in 1970 found that 41 percent of the water supplies of 969 randomly selected communities provided "inferior quality water." Nationwide surveys have indicated that over 400 different chemicals are to be found in tap water, and further work is being done on chlorine. Chlorine is the most common chemical used in municipal water supplies for purification, and studies are beginning to indicate that it has some possible long-term negative effects. Water experts further admit that we are only just beginning to understand how the organic and inorganic chemical substances present in water might eventually affect human beings.

However, most experts still believe that water in the United States is the best in the world. The United States is *not* facing a water emergency, but an ever-growing number of people aren't waiting around for one to be declared. Mineral water most often tastes better than what comes from a tap, and its purity can be depended upon.

Mineral water is also one of the earth's first medicines. There's no record of when the first dinosaur found relief from arthritis by dunking in a hot spring. And there's also no record of when the first human found relief from having eaten too much dinosaur by drinking from an effervescent pool. But there are records aplenty of the cures wrought at spas by mineral waters.

In fact, it's impossible to discuss mineral water *without* discussing spas. The history of the waters is so intermixed with legend, mysticism, and religion, and then so intermingled with medical science, that it's terribly difficult to separate it all. The Food and Drug Administration forbids therapeutic advertising claims for mineral waters sold in the United States, but great segments of the rest of the world still seek relief for what pains them by "taking the waters."

Europeans have used spa therapy for thousands of years for all the ills humankind is heir to—arthritis, excess of cholesterol, stomach, liver, kidney, and gall bladder disorders, heart and cardiovascular diseases, and so on. In France and most other European countries, academies of medicine, comparable to our own American Medical Association, study specific waters and specific ailments and make recommendations to ministries of health. With either our American sophistication or chauvinism in full sail, it's taken us some time to become seriously interested in theories so long practiced elsewhere.

Lithium, for example, is being hailed by many doctors today as a "miracle drug" in the treatment of certain emotional disorders. Far from being a new discovery, however, it is found in many mineral waters and was known and widely prescribed by Roman physicians. Certain other waters were renowned for clearing up skin conditions, and we know

now that these waters contain large amounts of sulfur—a chief ingredient of many modern acne remedies. Today, after a heavy meal, Americans either Plop, Plop, Fizz, Fizz, or chew a tablet composed mainly of bicarbonate of soda. Elsewhere, indigestion is relieved by imbibing an effervescent mineral water which also supplies the same bicarb. If we have a mineral deficiency, we either pop a pill, or get popped by a needle. Other people, however, supplement their mineral intake . . . with mineral water.

But if *all* water is mineral water, why not just go back to the tap to receive all these wonderful benefits? The answer is simple. Mineral water is *hard* water because of its mineral content. This may make it healthful to drink, but it also makes it lousy for washing hair because it won't produce suds. Municipalities therefore make their water soft by processing and treating it. This processing removes much of the water's mineral content, thereby helping the shampoo but lessening the possible therapeutic benefits.

But aside from the safety factor and possible curative powers of natu-

ral mineral water, it can also help with mineral balance. The human body is a very intricate chemistry lab. Using just a few raw materials, it makes all the things we need to stay active and healthy. Minerals are among the necessary raw materials and, conveniently, we need them in very small amounts. Most of the minerals we require are supplied by the food we eat, but since we are talking about waters, here is a short rundown on the minerals most usually found in them and the functions they serve in our bodies. (Note: When a water is mentioned later as being *high* in a certain mineral, don't be misled. What this actually means is that there is a higher concentration of one of the minerals present than the others. In terms of recommended daily mineral intake, one would usually have to drink many liters of a water to exceed the allowance.)

Calcium. Aside from its role in the formation of bones and teeth, calcium also helps with the maintenance of cell membranes. It is also required for nerve impulses, muscle contractions, and proper heartbeat rhythm. For a normal adult, the National Academy of Sciences recommends 800 milligrams per day.

Phosphorus. Necessary for the formation of compounds that store and release energy, phosphorus also plays a role in assuring that body fluids and tissues do not become too alkaline or too acid. A normal adult requires 800 milligrams daily.

Sodium (Salt). For many people, too much sodium can create problems. But we do need it to help our blood cells retain their proper amount of water (osmotic pressure). This explains why an excess of sodium results in the retention of too much water. It is not really known how much is required daily, but people on *restricted* diets achieve sodium balance with 500 milligrams.

Iron and **Copper.** These are essential for the formation of hemoglobin (the protein in the red blood cells that moves oxygen from the lungs to the tissues). Trace amounts are required each day.

Iodine. This mineral is needed for the proper functioning of the thyroid gland. And lots of things slow down if the thyroid does—heart rate, transmission of nerve impulses, thinking processes, and burning of food. The recommended intake per day is 130 micrograms (more as you get older).

Magnesium. Without enough magnesium (250 milligrams for men,

300 for women), depression is possible, as is muscular weakness, muscle cramps, and dizziness.

Zinc. Essential for the synthesis of body proteins and the actions of many enzymes, zinc also helps mobilize the system's vitamin A. Daily recommended intake is 12 milligrams.

Potassium. This mineral also helps with osmotic pressure, the transmission of nerve impulses, and muscle contractions. The exact requirements are not known, but daily food intake covers it in all but extreme cases.

Mineral waters may be helpful because of what they can *add* to the human body, but they are also valuable for what they can help it do without.

A Harris poll of October 1976 found Americans ranking "good health" highest on their list of priorities (regardless of age, education, or income). And only 14 percent of those surveyed believed that Americans ate the kinds of food necessary to keep them healthy. Furthermore, about four in ten agreed that their diets would be better balanced with a reduced intake of sugar, salt, and soft drinks. Suffice it to say, the replacement of even one sugary soft drink per day with a glass of natural mineral water certainly couldn't hurt.

So there are definitely positive health reasons for drinking mineral water. Aside from safety and curative properties, the waters can help balance mineral intake, and help you kick the sugar habit.

However, let's not discount the contribution of snob appeal to the growth of the mineral water industry. It is said that Ben Franklin, after finishing his stint as ambassador to France, was among the first Americans to import water from abroad. The ignominy of snobbishness should not be ascribed to Ben, but it sure can be ascribed elsewhere. It's now chic to ask for mineral water, and the more esoteric the better. What a high to outsnob a maître d' by asking for a chilled glass of Golden Eagle—and then condescending to inform him that the water is bottled in India and flows down in pristine purity from the high Himalayas.

In many fashionable restaurants, the three-martini lunch is fast being replaced by the three-Ramlösa lunch (with Evian ice cubes and an Apollinaris chaser).

And people are beginning to talk about the comparative taste of waters as they do about wines. Water tastings are held, and the seriousness with which they are taken bodes ill/well for the future, depending upon where you sit.

A list of words is in order now to help clarify some of the terms already mentioned and to introduce others that are to come. So with glass firmly in hand, welcome to *The Book of Waters*.

Mineral water, as we've said, can mean *any* water. The most famous of the bottled mineral waters just so happen to have a combination of minerals that please both the taste and the digestive system. (For delicate systems, such as babies', waters with a very low mineral content can help guard against stomach upset. This is why they are often recommended for formulas.) By the way, underground volcanic action, or the movement of huge underground rock formations, is thought to account for a water coming up hot, or not.

Natural spring water is mineral water that reaches the earth's surface without being pumped. Nothing is added to it and nothing is removed; it remains unprocessed in any way. It is bottled from springs that have usually been flowing for thousands of years and have no end in sight. The best domestic and imported waters issue from carefully protected sources with long-established reputations for consistency and purity.

Bottled water is a catch-all phrase. All you can be sure about with bottled water is that it's a version of H_2O and it's being carried home in a container of some kind. Nearly 80 percent of all bottled water sold in the United States is not natural. It is reprocessed tap water that has been treated, so learn to read labels carefully.

Treated water is also called "processed," "formulated," or "facsimile." This is water that has been processed, usually by an infusion of chemicals for purification or other reasons. It can also undergo an entire lexicon of unpronounceable treatments—deionization, reverse osmosis, electrolialysis, and distillation. In any case, if the water has been processed, the label, by law, must tip you off. Look for phrases like "spring-fresh" or "spring-pure." Only natural spring water can be called so. And the same is true for sparkling water. It cannot be called "naturally effervescent" if it's been gassed up artificially after leaving the spring.

Effervescent water, or "sparkling" or "carbonated" water, is naturally carbonated below the surface of the earth. It contains an excess of gas that makes bubbles while escaping at normal air temperature. Most of the bottlers capture the escaping gas and infuse it back into the water during the bottling process. This is fine and "natural" because the gas being added *to* the water is the gas *from* the water. It's interesting to note that when a water is naturally carbonated, the bubbles usually stay around longer than they do in artificially carbonated water.

Still water is simply water with no bubbles. Still waters do have gas in them (all water does), but the gas is in a dissolved state.

Well water, also called artesian well water, has to be pumped to the surface. It often must be processed in some way as well, to assure its purity. It is often very high in sulfates and chlorides, looks muddy, and tastes yucky.

Distilled water has been vaporized and then condensed back again to liquid. The result is water with *no* mineral content and therefore no taste. Most agree that its proper place is in a steam iron, car battery, or baby's formula, rather than in a drinking glass.

Hard water contains 100 parts or more of dissolved solids per million parts of water. Its mineral content is higher than that of soft water. This makes it more healthful to drink but lousy for washing your hair because it won't lather up. Most bottled mineral waters lean toward hardness.

Soft water lathers well, so most municipal water supplies strive to make their water soft. This is most often done by replacing the calcium and magnesium present with sodium, or salt. This makes the water soft all right, but it isn't so great for people who have to monitor their sodium intake. You can tell whether a water is soft, distilled, or hard by making ice cubes. Soft water will make cloudy cubes. Distilled water cubes will be crystal clear, and hard water cubes will sport a white spot in their center where all the minerals have huddled together.

pH factor is a chemist's term that indicates the level of acidity and alkalinity in a solution. Water, for example, that is neither acid nor alkaline is indicated by the pH number 7. This means that it is neutral. Numbers *below* 7 indicate acidity, and as the numbers drop from 7 to 1, the level of acidity rises. Numbers *above* 7 indicate alkalinity, and as the numbers rise, so does the alkaline level. Some mineral waters even come quite close to the pH of the human bloodstream—7.42.

Spa comes from the Lation *espa,* or fountain. The word has now taken on the generic sense of meaning any health resort. But in its more specific use, the word refers to places where water cures are offered. Extensive literature exists in Europe and elsewhere on specific ailments which are treatable by drinking and bathing in waters with specific mineral contents. And going to spas is not ancient history. Great numbers of people all over the world still flock to their favorite places for treatment, relaxation, entertainment, socializing, and just plain down-home vacationing.

Hydrotherapy is the general term for the treatment of disease by using water. Combine this with **balneology,** the science dealing with the therapeutic use of baths and bathing, add a dose of rest and relaxation—and you have spa therapy.

Diuretics help increase the amount of urine that passes through the body, thereby helping cleanse the system. Many mineral waters have diuretic properties.

PERHAPS APOCRYPHAL TALE #1 (as a reward for reading the definition of diuretic)

Noel Coward is said to have been invited to dinner one evening. After greeting his hostess, he announced his thirst. The woman scurried off and returned shortly with a glass of water. The redoubtable Coward is supposed to have looked at the glass of water, then back at the hostess, then back to the glass, and finally back to the hostess.

"I said I was thirsty," he remarked, "not dirty."

PERHAPS APOCRYPHAL TALE #2 (as a reward for reading Apocryphal Tale #1)

W. C. Fields often went on record as a man who never drank water. When asked why, he replied:

"I don't drink water because fish _____ in water."

(Note: Of the numerous choices available to Fields for filling in the blank, he is said to have chosen the word that added alliteration to the sentence.)

W.C. Fields, left, and Noel Coward: Don't drink the water!

Apollinaris

INE RUCKGABE
NO RETURN

ESTABLISHED OVER 100 YEARS

REGISTERED TRADE MARK

Apollinaris

The Queen of Table Waters

MINERAL W

WITH ITS OWN NATU

Entrance to the spring at Apollinaris

"The Queen of Table Waters" from Bad Neuenahr, West Germany. The water is naturally effervescent and is high in magnesium, sodium, and calcium. It is slightly alkaline, with a discernible presence and aftertaste.

The fertile plain bordering the Rhine River near Remagen was known for centuries as the Golden Mile. The Romans established colonies there and, according to legend, it was there that the Roman emperor Constantine had his famous "Vision of the Cross."

The Ahr Valley is located in the Golden Mile. Like its more famous neighbor the Rhine Valley, it has been producing wine for over 1,000 years. And were it not for the vineyards, it's quite possible that we wouldn't know of Apollinaris mineral water today.

In the middle of the nineteenth century, the Kreuzberg family had some trouble. They were among the most prosperous growers in the valley all right, but a number of their vines in the eastern part of the Ahr were withering. They attributed this to a lack of water, so Georg Kreuzberg decided an irrigation ditch was in order. He took shovel in hand in 1852 and dig he did. Very soon,

Emperor Constantine, above, with wreath and water; inset, the Ahr Valley

however, fumes arose from his ditch and then a geyser of clear, sparkling water shot into the air.

Interested in another version of the story? The vines are still withering in version two, but this time Georg takes a soil sample. He has it analyzed by a famed geologist and is told that the soil is inundated with carbonic acid gas. This could only be the result of a mineral spring in the area, and Georg is advised to dig a well. Dig he does again, and at the forty-foot level, Apollinaris water is finally freed from the confines of the earth.

Whatever actually happened, Georg tasted the water and found its flavor and sparkle to his liking. So he began to collect it for his family, friends, and the other growers in the area. The popularity of the water grew steadily. By this time, Georg was calling the water Apollinaris—after an old chapel dedicated to St. Apollinaris that stood at the foot of his vineyard.

Georg's brother-in-law lived in

The "wooded eminence known as Apollinarisberg"

England at the time and ran a small import business. After a visit to Germany, the relative brought some of the water home and gave it to a friend, a well-known newspaper publisher. Well, the publisher knew a good thing when he tasted it and suggested that negotiations begin for distribution rights. A deal was struck, and Apollinaris Company Limited was formed with its corporate base in London. Georg Kreuzberg agreed to gear up for more vigorous production and invested some of his front money in bottling equipment. Apollinaris Limited, in the meantime, actively commenced to export the water throughout England and to practically every country in the world. Export on this scale began in the late 1870s.

St. Apollinaris

On September 29, 1877, the *Illustrated London News* published a report filed by an English journalist who had traveled to the Ahr Valley. The prose is a bit purple, but obviously poetic affectation of the times required it. To wit:

Tourists up the Rhine always recall with pleasure the moment when its picturesque beauties first burst upon their view, and the splendid panorama formed by the ruin-crowned peaks of the romantic Siebengebirge, the scene of the redoubtable exploits of the legendary Siegfried. . . . Higher up the river, past

Rising up is an extensive range of buildings forming three sides of a square, with a tall chimney backed by vine-clad slopes towering aloft, and millions of glass and stone bottles in gigantic stacks occupying the central space. Workpeople are moving briskly about, while a procession of huge carts, the lading of which is just completed, is preparing to start on the road to the Rhine.

The anonymous reporter then goes on to describe the bottling operations, which were replete with a *half score of Lieschens and Lottchens*

The Lieschens *and* Lottchens *at work*

the shattered walls of Rolandseck and the shady green islet of Nonnenwerth, the cloistered retreat of the betrothed bride of the brave Roland when

> 'False tidings reached the
> Rhenish strand
> That he had fallen in fight'

there rises up on the right bank of the river a beautifully wooded eminence known as Apollinarisberg. Crowning its summit is the Apollinaris Kirche, a handsome modern Gothic edifice. . . . It is decorated with some admirable frescoes of incidents in the life of St. Apollinaris, whose remains are here enshrined in an antique sarcophagus, and who is the patron saint not only of the church, but of a special crystal spring which gushes out of the limestone rock. . . .

Make you thirsty?

The visitor then comes across the bustle of the Apollinaris bottling facility, nestled "in the heart of this sequestered valley."

with looped-up petticoats and kerchief-covered heads who were clustered around an apparatus not unlike a huge cart-wheel. . . . From each of its four and twenty spokes shot up a peculiar jet of water, and on these jets the girls were deftly slipping and removing the bottles. . . . Four thousand bottles were thus being rinsed per hour, or from forty to fifty thousand per diem.

Wishing next to view the spring, our reporter discovers that its romantic beauty has been sacrificed to the necessity of enclosing it.

On descending a flight of steps at the back of the filling room, we reached a small inner court impregnated with a strong odour of carbonic acid gas, issuing in volumes from the spring and confined in a large metal reservoir. The gas does, nevertheless, escape considerably, and is sometimes so overpowering, that it is impossible to descend the steps. . . . Fifty feet below the surface is the spring itself, which wells up some

Taking the sun in Bad Neuenahr

twenty feet, and is there met by four supply pumps and the machinery specially erected to recondense the gas into the water prior to the latter being pumped into the bottlingroom. Thus the strong effervescence for which Apollinaris is remarkable is attained without admixture of any foreign ingredient. The artificial chemistry of the laboratory vainly endeavors to rival the refined operations of Nature.

His final shot is a public relations dream and leads one to paranoid musings about the possible connections between the anonymous journalist and the "well-known newspaper publisher" who now, coincidentally, happens to be heavily invested in a water company.

The Appolinaris water, springing forth from its deep, rocky source, clear as crystal, soft as velvet, and effervescent as champagne, is not only of the highest purity, but preserves its sparkling freshness longer than any artificially aerated water.

Before the turn of the century and up until about 1914, sales of Apollinaris were growing nicely. Advertising pitched the water as the perfect mixer for scotch, whiskey, and bourbon, and for additional use as ice cubes.

Part of the popularity of Apollinaris at this time was the woeful condition of many of the world's natural water supplies. One bout with typhoid made investing in Apollinaris on a daily basis look like

a bargain. The journalist obviously couldn't have agreed more. He remarks in the same article:
Ordinary drinking water and many aerated waters, although to the eye transparent and sparkling, are "magazines of disease," leading to diarrhoea, fever, and various forms of blood poisoning.

And, perhaps, while the memory of a just-consumed steak and kidney pie was fresh in his mind, he wrote: "medical men assert that [Apollinaris's] anti-acid properties successfully combat the dyspeptic conditions to which English stomachs are particularly liable."

The idyllic tale of the company's growth came to a crashing halt with the outbreak of World War I in 1914. It became impossible for the British Apollinaris company to import any of the water from Germany, and after the war ended, it took a very long time for business to get back to normal. Good will, as one can easily imagine, was not the prevailing mood of the day. Slowly but surely, however, the company began to achieve its pre-war success. Then World War II arrived—and it all came crashing down again.

After the war, efforts were made to start over once more, but the face of the world had changed substantially. Various assets of the British company had been sold off and it took years for the restructure and reorganization of Apollinaris to take place. But take place they did, and today Apollinaris belongs to the top four producers in Europe and is expanding constantly. The company recently built a new bottling plant, for example, which they call the largest in the world. It has a capacity of 120,000 liters per hour, and can do over 500 million per year. Apollinaris now exports to 45 countries and employs 450 people.

The curative properties of the water have figured prominently in the company's advertising through the years, and recent European promotional materials include the following.

These complaints or maladies are especially benefited by the use of Apollinaris Water:
1. In cases of Acute and Chronic Dyspepsia (Gastric and Intestinal Catarrh) the regular use of Apollinaris Water is attended with great improvement.
2. Catarrhal affections of the Throat and Respiratory Organs (Acute and Chronic Laryngeal and Bronchial Catarrh). In these cases, Apollinaris Water, especially when mixed with one-fourth as much boiling milk, promotes expectoration, soothes the membranes of the respiratory membrane, eases the cough, and gives general relief.
3. Calculous affections and Catarrhal disorders of the Urinary organs, associated with Uric acid gravel and gouty states. Relief is afforded by the alkaline, solvent, and diuretic properties of Apollinaris Water.

The therapeutic claims for Apollinaris, as for most of the European waters, are quite serious. The company has conducted extensive clinical studies on how the waters can aid in the cure of such maladies as chronic constipation, disorders due to irritant laxatives, occasional constipation, dyskinetic gall bladder, and dyspeptic orders associated with diabetes. The most recent of these studies, as a matter of fact, was published in 1976.

Apollinaris has a high sodium, magnesium, and calcium content which has remained relatively stable over the years. Analyses done in 1933, 1961, and 1973 showed that the composition of the water had remained virtually the same.

The water cure: good for what ails you

From Saint Galmier, France. The water is naturally effervescent and light in minerals. Almost sodium-free, with calcium, magnesium—and fluoride! It is lightly alkaline with sprightly bubbles.

Well, if it was good enough for Gilles Gorrozet in 1539, it should be good enough for anyone. Gilles, in fact, liked Badoit so much he said it's "perhaps more delicious than a beautiful wine." And for an authentic, card-carrying Frenchman, that's quite a statement.

Looks as if the Romans liked it as

well. Recent excavations near the site of the spring uncovered baths. And if the Romans were dipping themselves in the stuff, it's likely they also took a swig or two.

The Badoit spring is in the Loire Valley, in the thirteenth-century town of Saint Galmier. Saint Galmier is in the Lyon mountain range, quite near the Alps.

The waters of Badoit rise from a natural spring that sits atop a water table some 1,500 feet underground. It moves upward through heavy layers of blue granite and other minerals until it reaches the surface. It is lightly enough carbonated so that you won't feel bloated after drinking it.

And another gift from Ol' Mother Nature is fluoride. Yes, fluoride, as in "Why is little Johnny brushing his teeth with that funny orange toothpaste, Sarah Jane?" "Because it has fluoride, Grandpa, and his checkups have been just fine."

The fluoride content of Badoit is 1.2 parts per million (which the company calls "an ideal amount"). There is, however, no literature concerning how much Badoit you have to drink, gargle, or swish around in your mouth to avoid tooth decay and have good checkups like little Johnny. On the better-safe-than-sorry front, though, French parents have been known to encourage their own "petits Jeans" to drink the water regularly.

Badoit is collected and bottled just as it emerges from the earth. The process is fully automated and the bottling plant is actually pressurized so that no outside air can enter and affect the water's natural carbonation.

Badoit was recommended by doctors of the Loire as early as the 1600s. It is low in sodium and rich in calcium and magnesium.

Try it as a nonalcoholic nightcap. It's noncaloric, unflavored, and nicely bubbled. Also, chill your Badoit before serving. If you pour it *warm* over ice, the effervescence will escape much more quickly. And when you use it as a mixer, follow these steps: First, put the ice in the glass; then, add the hooch of your choice; and, finally, pour in the chilled Badoit. The water's sloshing into the glass is all the stirring that's needed. All you'll do by mixing additionally is force the gas out of the water, thereby lessening the life and taste of your drink.

And Badoit will also improve the taste of that 39¢-a-quart wine you bought when you saw how badly overdrawn you were. The bubbles and mineral balance seem to cut the bitterness.

SPARKLING
MINERAL WATER
BRU
bottled at the Spring
by s.a. Compagnie Générale de Chevron
4081 Chevron BELGIUM
NET 33 FL. OZ (1 QT. 1 Q

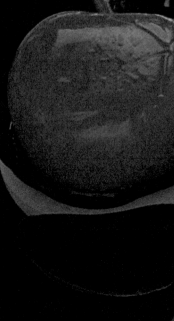

MERCI
DANK U
REBOUCHEZ-MOI, MEME VIDE - LEGE FLES HERSLUITEN A.U.B.

An effervescent water from Chevron, Belgium. It has a pH of 6.5 to 7.0, moderate sodium, calcium, and magnesium content, and a soft, neutral flavor.

Quite a guy, that Peter the Great. In 1710, he was so enamored of the waters of Bru, and found them to be so beneficial for his stomach, that he drank twenty-one glasses every morning. What he did next was eat twelve figs and six pounds of cherries and then take "straight to his feet for a walk."

Historical documentation about Bru goes back a good deal earlier than Peter the Great, however. In the fourth century A.D., Roman maps indicated an "acid fountain" (carbonated spring) in what is now the town of Chevron. In 814, the spring was being exploited in a rudimentary fashion and was given over to the new principality of Stavelot-Malmédy by Louis the Pious (the son of Charlemagne). And in the sixteenth century, the waters of Chevron were used by the local monks for what ailed them. Production on an industrial scale began in 1903, with the formation of the company involved with Bru to this day.

The Bru spring is located in the Liège province of Belgium, in the Ardennes region. The water is safeguarded by a boundary which was established by royal decree in 1934. The decree stated that the waters of Bru were to be used for the benefit of the public and therefore any

Peter the Great

Peter's repast

Louis the Pious
(son of Charlemagne)

It is therefore an ideal drink for the sick or those convalescing, for young girls with pale complexions [.!], for men who have overindulged in the consumption of alcoholic beverages and tobacco, and for those suffering the ill effects of overspiced foods. . . .

The waters of Bru warmed or with the chill taken off can act as a mild laxative.

The Bru bottling facility nestles quite comfortably smack in the middle of an evergreen forest and looks, from the air, very like a resort hotel.

During the collecting process, the natural gas already present in the water is drawn off. It is compressed, liquefied, and stored in tanks. Then, during the bottling process, the carbonation is reinjected into the water. This is done in carefully monitored amounts to assure uniformity.

work in the area that might reduce the flow of the spring or contaminate the waters was prohibited.

Naturally, curative properties have been ascribed to the waters. The translation of an old brochure states:

According to the most reputed experts in hygiene, and physicians who have come to know the beneficial effects of Bru waters, these waters constitute an unrivaled drink for people whose stomachs are delicate or have been spoiled by gastronomic excesses.

Bru water prevents the numerous ailments which can afflict the stomach and enables food to be properly absorbed by ensuring perfect digestion.

From Caddo Valley, Arkansas. A still water with a neutral pH (7.0). Very low in sodium and high in calcium. A light, clear taste.

The Caddo Valley Spring is located in the western part of the Ouachita range (a part of the Ozarks) in the Ouachita National Forest. The forest embraces 1.5 million acres of mountains, ridges, lakes, and streams and sprawls from central Arkansas into southeast Oklahoma.

The spring itself is in a deep valley and is almost completely surrounded by government-owned land.

The formal history of Caddo Valley began in 1541 when Hernando de Soto came up against some angry Tula Indians there. (The explorer fared a whole lot better with the Caddos and the Quapaws, as you will see in the section on Mountain Valley water.)

To this day, Caddo Valley is listed as Cox Spring on all the maps. The name it carries is that of William J. Cox, a man who homesteaded forty acres (including the spring) just after the end of the Civil War. Although in a rather remote area, the spring still managed to attract its share of romance—and tragedy. The tale goes like this: William had a wife and also a younger brother, John Randolph Cox. John, unfortunately as it turned out, had a crush on William's wife and made some serious advances when his older brother was away. The wife, however, spurned John. In a fit of rage, he killed her with an ax, leaving her infant daughter crying beside the body. John was caught and hung for his crime. The little girl, named Damey, grew up at the spring and died there, never having married.

Today, Caddo Valley is owned by Mrs. E. Harnik of Hot Springs, Arkansas. Mrs. Harnik provided background that was as charming as it was informative. This is her response to a question about the geological age of the springs: "Well, as my one-hundred-year-old uncle would say, 'You'll have to ask someone older than me!' He should know a lot about the area as he married a girl 'Cox,' a niece of the homesteader William J. Cox."

Mrs. Harnik goes on to describe the development of the area. "Although the spring has always been privately owned, travelers have considered it *their* spring. They came in wagons with fruit jars and syrup jugs—even tubs. Now they come in Cadillacs with plastic five-gallons, Gallo wine bottles—you name it, I've seen it. It's free, and they know it always will be." (Note: Although the Caddo Valley Spring is very much a business—two million gallons were shipped last year to Texas, Oklahoma, and Kansas—water is still free at the source to travelers and visitors.)

Spanish soldiers in the New World

Melvin A. Dickins holds the lease to the spring and provides additional background: "I drove 42 miles to deliver my first four bottles. Today we have twelve trucks and twenty-one employees, and have had an increase in sales every year for twenty-six years. . . . Ten years of kidney trouble put me in the business accidentally."

The mention of Mr. Dickins's kidney troubles prompted a question: Does Caddo Valley water have any therapeutic values? "For a hangover," replied Mrs. Harnik. "Drink several glasses—it's light-bodied and easy to drink. It'll keep you running, but it will dilute the alcohol and make you feel better faster."

Other uses? "Use Caddo Valley for cooking, for tea, coffee, mixed drinks. Though you might not taste the difference, it is water that has not been drunk before, or used before, and your body will know the difference."

Scientific? No. But as my one-hundred-year-old uncle used to say . . .

NATURAL MINERAL WATER

FAMOUS SINCE 1760

"*the water of aware french women*"
DECLARED OF PUBLIC INTEREST AUTHORIZATION OF JUNE 22nd 1861

ConTREXÉVILLE

from the Pavillon spri~~ng~~

BOTTLED BY SOCIÉTÉ GÉNÉRALE DE GRANDES SOURCES ~~DE~~
CONTREXÉVILLE (VOS~~GES~~

NET 34 FL. O~~Z.~~ ~~3~~ FL. OZ.)

In the garden at Contrexéville (1864)

A still water from Contrexéville, France, with a ph of 7.0, high in calcium and magnesium and low in sodium. It is promoted as "The Water of Aware Women," but many feel it to be an acquired taste. One could as easily call it "interesting" as "medicinal."

Louis Guilgot and Joseph Hilaire were among the earliest recorded fans of Contrexéville because in the eighteenth century they were the first two people cured at the spa under medical supervision. Up until that time, however, the waters of Contrex were a pretty well kept secret. They even seemed to escape completely the notice of the Romans. Although certain linguists maintain that the name Contrexéville derived from the Roman *Contra Aquas Villa*, there is no evidence in the form of ruins or artifacts that would confirm a Roman presence at the site.

In fact, the waters must have been a *very* well kept secret because Montaigne passed very close to Contrex without knowing of its existence. Then, in the middle of the eighteenth century, along came King Stanislas Leczinski of Poland (or to be more precise, ex-king Stanislas, since he was in exile at the time). Exile or not, Stanislas somehow managed the good fortune to marry off daughter Marie to King Louis XV. And, since mama didn't raise no fool, the first thing that Stanislas did after assuring himself of Louis's intentions was borrow a very large sum of money. Happy days were here again, and the generous pension bestowed by Louis iced the cake. Stanislas lived quite well, thank you.

Stanislas Leczinski, father-in-law

Louis XV, son-in-law

A Dr. Bagard was Stanislas's personal physician at the time, and the good doctor was sent to the springs of Contrexéville in 1750 after Stanislas heard of their curative properties. What the doctor found upon arriving was a pretty little village in the heart of a valley, situated in the middle of two branches of the river

Louis XVI, not a crowd pleaser

Deverre. He wrote: "It is in the center of this island in the middle of a green and lush garden that one finds at the edge of the village the mineral spring." After the doctor made his analysis of the properties of the water, he further commented, "What a happy discovery for the human race."

Dr. Bagard later wrote an extensive treatise on the waters and explained in great detail all of the illnesses (some of which seem very odd) and all of the cures (some of which seem very miraculous) wrought at the spa.

For many years, though, the reputation of Contrex remained local, and the cures were not particularly organized. It took the visit of a Dr. Thouvenel to cause the building of the first real treatment center. The doctor was the personal physician of Louis XVI and visited in 1774 under direction of the inspector general of the mineral waters of France. Doctor Thouvenel analyzed the waters once more and reaffirmed the existence and value of their curative properties. He also set down the first stone for the building of the treatment center. Contrexéville was on its way.

Since the burgeoning spa had the personal endorsement of the king himself, it became an important place. The nobility started to arrive, as did members of the wealthy merchant class. The king's brother even had a villa built for himself at Contrex. Many English came as well. In fact, one of the city's hotels was called by locals "the house of the English."

The French Revolution, however, took much of the wind from Contrexéville's sails, and the First Empire all but neglected it. It wasn't until the last years of the Second Empire that Contrex again found itself in vogue. In 1865, an important financial group acquired the spring and started modernizing immediately. But as a chronicler of the times wrote, there were still no casinos and no theaters—the only distractions were the cure-seekers themselves and artists who happened to be passing through.

But by the end of the nineteenth century, Contrex had beautiful parks and buildings and was known as one of Europe's most comfortable spas. And it drew the cream of society, including some early Rothschilds, the Marquis of Salisbury (who would ride through the streets of Contrex on his tricycle), and Queen Isabel of Spain (whose frequent and tumultuous love affairs were the toast of the town).

Another interesting visitor was the shah of Persia, who arrived in 1900 dressed in a diamond vest, gleaming saber, glittering necklaces, and carrying a brace of eagles. The shah had heard of Contrexéville and took his royal self and his royal kidney stones to check it out. Participating in the checking out was the shah's entire family, a gaggle of advisers, a number of bodyguards, an army of servants, a passel of court favorites, and just about every living Persian resident of Europe. Contrex was turned overnight into a suburb of Tehran and someone at the time wrote that one could not move without bumping into a Persian. There were, of course, compensating factors. The shah spent over 100,000 francs on trifles during his stay—tips and little gifts for his entourage. Upon his departure, he sent a warm telegram expressing his satisfaction with the spa and, as it turns out, returned two more times in the ensuing years.

Contrexéville faces south in the Vosges Mountains, very near the German border. The spa itself is over 1,100 feet above sea level and is open from late May through early October. It offers all the expected distractions and even has two artificial lakes about a mile away, one for fishing and the other for swimming and sailing.

The source that yields the bottled water is the best known of the eight springs of Contrex. It spews out 44,000 gallons of very cold water daily, which add up to the over 450 million bottles sold yearly. The waters of Contrexéville have been prescribed by European physicians for hundreds of years—especially for geriatric and urinary problems. Contrex calls itself the most diuretic of all the diuretic waters and is used widely by French women to counteract "water fatness." This traditional use of the water is what prompted the company's slogan, "The Water of Aware Women."

The Marquis of Salisbury, with tricycle

100,000 francs on trifles; Muzaffer-Ed-Din-Murza, the Shah of Persia

DEER PARK®

100%
Spring Water

NET 64 FL OZS (½ GAL.)

From the Nestlé Company, White Plains, New York. This still water has a pH of 7.4 and a low sodium content. The taste is variously described as soft, simple, clean—or bland. (Also available in a sparkling form with added carbonation.)

Deer Park water originally came from the Deer Park Spa in the crest of the Alleghenies in western Maryland—a summer resort which was built in 1873. The attraction of the area was its bracing mountain air, beautiful views, and abundant pure

glass. Part of the appeal of this type of packaging is the heat-sealed cap. The inner liner of the cap becomes fused to the mouth of the jug during the bottling process. This liner has to be punctured or peeled away before you can get at the water. If *you* can't get at the water, so the reasoning goes, then neither can germs.

And here's a new one for you—"spiked" water. Try it between courses at dinner to refresh the palates of all the gourmets at table.

James Garfield, Grover Cleveland, Benjamin Harrison, William Taft

spring water. Deer Park quickly became popular and attracted four American presidents—Cleveland, Harrison, Garfield, and Taft. Not surprisingly, Deer Park became known soon after as "The Spa of the Presidents."

Servicing the resort was the B&O Railroad, which served Deer Park water (with its "delightful and palatable taste") to all the patrons of its plush dining cars.

When Nestlé bought the company, they moved from the first source to another close by that yields water with a parallel profile to the original. (Nothing underhanded involved, mind you; the water remains 100 percent spring water.)

One benefit of a giant like Nestlé owning the company is the marvelous quality control that is brought to the product. Daily samples are drawn and analyses made to assure the water's purity and uniformity.

Deer Park is sold in gallon and half-gallon plastic jugs. The plastic doesn't seem to impart any taste to the water, and it *is* lighter than

For each 2 cups of chilled Deer Park, add one of the following:
1 teaspoon vanilla extract *or*
½ **teaspoon orange extract** *or*
½ **teaspoon lemon extract** *or*
¼ **teaspoon mint extract** *or*
¼ **teaspoon anise extract.**
Pour the ingredients into a pitcher with Deer Park ice cubes. Stir and serve. (NOTE: Neither this writer nor the Nestlé Company will be held accountable should you decide to mix all the extracts together. It would be interesting, however, to know what happens to you.)

A storage tip is to refrain from leaving Deer Park in an open pitcher in the fridge. It will pick up food odors and the taste will be spoiled. Also, try using the water to crisp carrot curls and radishes, and sprinkle some of it lightly on top of store-bought French bread before popping it in the oven (it will help brown the top).

And a few of the more whimsical uses for the water suggested by the company are to moisten your postage stamps with it, water your lawn with it, wash your diamonds in it, and use it to fill your water bed (now, that's inconspicuous consumption of the first order!).

ESTAB. 1895
EPHRATA
DIAMOND
SPRING
WATER
TRADE   MARK

BOTTLE TO BE RETURNED
WHEN EMPTY TO
EPHRATA DIAMOND
SPRING WATER CO
EPHRATA PA

Ephrata Diamond

From Ephrata, Pennsylvania. A still water with a light mineral content and a soft, unaggressive flavor.

Ephrata sits about in the middle of Pennsylvania, and about in the middle of the middle of Pennsylvania Dutch country. The Ephrata Diamond Spring Water Company is the lone survivor of six water companies that, over the years, called Ephrata home.

Ephrata itself has an interesting history. It began as a community of German Pietists who sought to live their lives differently from their neighbors. Their values were purity, culture, and industry—but *apart* from the rest of the world. The spa that was later built there drew people from all over, but only one hotel remains today as evidence of the area's popularity. The hotel is now called Mountain Springs and is operated as a retreat for people of the Spiritualist faith.

The history of the region as a source for mineral water began in 1895, when a man named Herr found a spring in a sandy area south of Ephrata. He liked the taste of the water very much and imagined that others would as well. So he filled a few milk cans and hawked his wares on the streets of nearby Lancaster. The water was fine but the operation was a little short on convenience: Herr's customers had to bring their own containers. (No deposit, all right, but you had to return if you wanted more water.)

Business was brisk, and when trucks came into use, Herr started bottling operations at the spring. In time, delivery routes were established and the spring was on its way.

The business eventually passed into the hands of another family, and that's when Ephrata's version of "a-feudin', a-fussin', and a-fightin' " began. Two more springs were discovered on the property, but instead of delighting in their expanded resources, the family set about cutting each other's economic throats. Attempts were made to pirate the springs by digging wells nearby to siphon off the water before it reached the surface. This had to

It started with milk cans

have ended badly, so a collective sigh of relief whispered around Ephrata when a nephew bought out his two relatives and combined the businesses.

At the time that the company was bought by Edwin A. Hess in 1944, peace had long since been restored and the company had three trucks and five employees.

Edwin Hess (father, by the way, of the current owner) started off in the shoe manufacturing business. He had, in fact, invented machines that aided in the manufacture of women's footwear. His journey from shoes to water was motivated by him overhearing a chance remark made by an employee of the water company. The remark, unfortunately, is lost to posterity, but the company is still very much with us.

Current operations stem from a 25,000-square-foot bottling plant a short distance from the springs themselves. The water is pumped into glass-lined tanks which are then transported to the plant in stainless steel tractor trailers. Present sources are the three aforementioned springs, which are surrounded by over 100 acres of mountains and woodlands. The land surrounding the springs is primarily sandstone, which acts as the water's natural filtration system.

From Evian-les-Bains, France. A slightly alkaline still water with a pH of 7.18. Evian has a moderate mineral content and is virtually sodium-free. It has a full, rounded, clear, and fresh flavor and is said to be the best-selling water in the world.

Evian-les-Bains has enjoyed an international reputation as a spa for over 200 years. And not hurting the town one bit is its location. It overlooks Lake Geneva in the high Alps and is almost opposite Lausanne, Switzerland.

The Evian Cachat spring is fed by waters which make a long and very slow journey. Part of the source is rainwater which falls on the uppermost peaks of the Mont Blanc range. That water joins the snow that covers the mountains, and both gradually seep into the ground to form a vast "water sheet." From there, the water trickles toward Evian through a huge filter of sandy masses of ice sitting between two layers of hard clay which shield the water from all external impurities. The spring maintains virtually the same water flow, temperature, and mineral content. (In fact, the physical-chemical composition of the water hasn't changed since the first analysis was done, over 100 years ago.)

The French Revolution began in 1789, but to one nobleman, Marquis de Lesert, the trouble in his kidneys was more important than the trouble in the streets. So off he went to the springs of Bas-Chablais for a cure. He still had his miseries after some time there, but one day he found himself on the slopes of Evian, near the garden belonging to a Monsieur Cachat. The marquis noticed some running water and, being thirsty, took a drink. He liked the taste so much that he came back regularly to quench his thirst. The Marquis's kidney stones disappeared, though the Revolution continued.

In 1859/60, things started to get a bit organized. The Société Anonyme des Eaux Minérales d'Evian was formed. At that time, the spa boasted a drinking hall, bathing rooms, and a small bottling plant for local water sales. In 1878, how-

Evian-les-Bains

From the Alps to the spring to the surface

ever, the French minister of health authorized the development of the spring after reviewing a favorable report from the French Academy of Medicine. Then things started to percolate.

The twentieth century brought a building boom. The bathing rooms were enlarged and christened the Hotel Splendide. (Today, the stainless steel pipes that carry the water from the spring to the bottling plant reside in the Splendide's basement.) A casino was constructed as well, as was a golf course, and the Hotel Royal, one of Europe's most

famous. Most of the buildings still stand, with the exception, alas, of the drinking hall.

Evian was doing something right. It drew the Aga Khan, Morocco's King Hassan, King Farouk, and England's Prime Minister Bevin. When the PM stayed in Evian, Scotland Yard came as well, and established a "branch office" in the lovely park which surrounds the Royal.

But another famous visitor suffered a terrible loss during his stay at the spa. Seems that there was a fire on the top floor of the Royal in 1958 while Errol Flynn was a guest. Everyone got out unharmed, but the flames consumed the swashbuckler's beloved collection of neckties.

Evian's sales have grown prodi-

The Aga Khan

giously over the years: from 8 million liters in 1948, to 447 million in 1964, to 800 million in the late 1970s. The nearly 80 million liters exported yearly by Evian make it the leading exporter of mineral waters in the world.

The major market for the water is still France, but Evian is to be found in eighty-three other countries as well: Belgium, Switzerland, and Italy in Europe; North and South America, and the Far East. Oh, and here's a reassuring note. Next time you get thirsty on the island of Malta, you can quench with Evian.

The therapeutic properties of the water also have a long history. The water is diuretic because it is easily absorbed and quickly assimilated. (It has been said that Evian is of greater value "for what it takes away than for what it brings.") And an absence of sodium makes the water safe for those on salt-free diets. But this is all minor league

English Prime Minister Ernest Bevin

King Farouk

stuff compared to how Evian is promoted in countries that allow therapeutic advertising. Evian is recommended for diseases of the kidneys, gout, arthritis, excess of cholesterol, allergic dermatosis, and eczema, among many, many others. Although Evian is sold in the United States simply as a delicious, naturally pure table water, it is used for its curative values by a great many people elsewhere.

Evian is also recommended for baby bottles because of its low mineral content and its purity. In addition, its low pH does not change the constitution of milk, and the water is said to facilitate digestion because of its infusion of oxygen, carbonic acid, calcium, and magnesium.

The Evian people also recommend the water for use in skin care. You can mist or wash with it, or use it with compresses. Seems that the neutral pH does not destroy the protective acidity of the skin, and the low mineral content does not congest it.

A last note: For the sleep-easy-at-night column, here are a few interesting reassurances from French law as it relates to natural mineral waters like Evian. In the first place, "natural mineral water" is actually a title that can only be awarded after an O.K. by the Ministry of Public

Bottling Evian

Health and the French Academy of Medicine. And there are some further requirements. It is necessary:

1. That the waters possess therapeutic virtues proved by long experience and supported by medical reports.
2. That there is full security from the chemical and bacteriological points of view (both at the source and during collecting and bottling).
3. That the physico-chemical content of the water is constant.
4. That there is a "safety perimeter" of land around the spring.
5. That nothing can be added to the water as it comes from the spring.
6. That periodic tests be conducted at laboratories appointed by the Ministry of Public Health.

So you see, Big Brother *is* watching—but in this case, he's a French bureaucrat and he seems benevolent.

Errol Flynn, sans *tie*

44

Fachingen

From Fachingen, West Germany. This effervescent water is high in sodium, calcium, and magnesium and has a pH of 6.1. The taste is very soft and light.

The next four weeks are supposed to work wonders. For this purpose I hope to be favored with Fachingen water and a sage wine, the one to liberate the genius, the other to inspire it.

—From a letter written by Goethe in 1843

That's what you call your basic heavyweight testimonial. And if one could be guaranteed that genius of Goethe's stripe would be liberated by drinking Fachingen, I would suggest that the other water companies fold their tents and quietly slip off into the night.

The origins of Fachingren are quite humble. Actually, a boatman from the river Lahn first drank the water in hopes of being cured of a lingering and obviously uncomfortable constipation. He recovered and told his colleagues about it. Others tried it to good result, and soon the boatmen were spreading the word up and down the river, praising Fachingen as "being better than all medicines."

All of this occurred in the first centuries of the Christian era. Remainders of very primitive well constructions have been unearthed at the site and dated.

The spring, however, stayed unknown for quite some time because of its relatively inaccessible location. It sits in a meadow in the midst of high mountains. (This perhaps accounts for the fact that Fachingen never became a spa.)

Even though the water provided cures for many, it was not all that pure in the beginning years of its use. Early inhabitants removed much of the earth and stone barriers that surrounded the spring and allowed the waters of Fachingen to mix with other, less pure waters— most of which had the Lahn River as their source.

In 1746, however, the barriers were reconstructed, and the purity of the spring was again protected against alien waters. The protective barriers were reinforced in 1823, and at the beginning of this century, the source of the spring was rechanneled to guard against the effects of the river once and for all.

Today, the German Health Department monitors Fachingen, assuring not only that the water is pure, but also that no chemical additives of any kind are introduced. The water bottled in Fachingen is in its pure and natural state.

In 1746, Dr. Forell, a noted physician of the time, first analyzed the water. He found its properties to be of benefit in the treatment of certain maladies and called it "one of the best German mineral waters." The first scientific treatise on the water was published in 1749, and since then, Fachingen has been pre-

Goethe

scribed for various ailments.

The town of Fachingen is located centrally in the West German state of Rheinland-Pfalz. The surrounding region is quite charming, offering idyllic valleys and the picture-postcard meanderings of the Lahn River.

The von Siemens family has managed the spring since 1894. The founder of the operation, Werner von Siemens, saw a natural tie-in between the mineral waters and the bottles he produced in his glass factory. Today, the spring is state-owned.

Over the years, the water has been especially recommended for indigestion and heartburn, gout, and bladder and kidney troubles. The company's tagline is: *"Fachingen State Springs Water Keeps the Body and Mind Healthy and Whole!"*

The sum-up, however, belongs to Goethe, who called Fachingen *"the emancipator of the spirit."*

BOTTLED AS REQUIRED BY MODERN SCIE
NATURAL MINERAL WATER
PRODUCT OF ITALY
FIUGGI
BOTTLED BY ENTE FIUGGI S.P.A.
UGGI - ITALY
L. OZ.

From Fiuggi, Italy. This still water has a very low mineral content and is virtually sodium-free. If anything, it is highest in calcium, and the water's taste can be described as either delicate . . . or flat.

Fiuggi water may indeed taste flat, but in 1299, Pope Boniface VIII was much too sick to care. In fact, someone wrote in a letter that "Nothing is left of Boniface save his eyes and tongue; for the rest, his whole body is putrefied." Kidney stones were plaguing Boniface and they probably would have killed him were it not for the arrival of a new personal physician who recommended the waters of Fiuggi. Vatican records show 187 payments made to the pope's personal envoys who shuttled back and forth between Rome and Fiuggi fifty-one times between the years 1299 and 1302. The treatment was a rousing success. The pope recovered so completely that we find this in a letter

Michelangelo

sent to the bishop of Valencia: "Our Pope is today young and healthy."

But if that's not recommendation enough, the waters of Fiuggi also relieved the suffering of one of the world's creative geniuses, Michelangelo. In 1548 it was written of him: "The indefatigable craftsman, who handled and carved so many stones, only just escaped death from a tiny stone that formed treacherously inside his aging body." The malady? Gallstones. The treatment? Fiuggi water. Michelangelo himself wrote on March 15, 1549: "I have been very ill, groaning night and day, unable to sleep or get any rest whatever. As far as they can make out, the doctors say I'm suffering from

Pope Boniface III

the stone." The Fiuggi treatment then began, and Michelangelo wrote one month later: "I am very much better to the wonderment of everyone because I had been taken for dead and myself believed the same." And two weeks later: "I am much better than I have been. Morning and evening I have been drinking the water from a spring about forty miles from Rome, which breaks up the stone. . . . I have had to lay in a supply at home and cannot drink or cook with anything else."

Movie stars' television commercials are one thing, but endorsements from a pope and Michelangelo carry *real* weight.

In 1666, the reputation of the

water had caused it to travel quite far afield. A letter of the time tells us: "The water of [Fiuggi] has been brought not only to Rome, Naples, Sicily, Sardinia, and Venice, but also to lands still further distant, such as France, Spain, and England."

But it wasn't all peaches and cream for Fiuggi. In 1870, a famous physician registered a complaint that left us not only with an interesting picture of a time and place, but also with insight into the fact that certain things are forever—like foot-dragging bureaucracy.

About a mile from the village of [Fiuggi] a perpetual mineral spring is to be found . . . there is no building of any sort in the vicinity, and thus visitors must shelter under the trees for protection against the rays of the sun. This notwithstanding during the hot season . . . a great throng of people flocks there to drink the water . . . it is hoped that someday the Municipal Authorities will shake themselves out of their lethargy, both in their own interest and in that of the many who need to make recourse to those waters which are so famed for their health-restoring powers, and build there some sort of convenient construction and also make the road less unpleasant.

Fiuggi lies about 40 miles southeast of Rome and about 75 miles from Naples. The spa is in the heart of the region of Lazio, about 2,500 feet above sea level, overlooking the river Sacco. The view is lovely, with mountains to the north, east, and west, and the region offers clean, bracing air, and a dry, mild climate. The spa is open from May until late October and has room for about 10,-000 visitors. The medieval village of Fiuggi that perches atop the hill is no less an attraction than the more modern pleasures of golf, tennis, and the like which await below.

Actually, the town has been called Fiuggi only since 1911. Fiuggi was always the name of the mineral spring, but the town itself was called Anticoli (the name that appears in the Vatican records and in the correspondence of Michelangelo). On August 10, 1911, however, royal decree made things a good deal simpler by calling the spa and the spring by the same name.

Fiuggi al fresco

The derivation of the name Fiuggi is not really known. Some suggest it to be from the Latin *filix,* or fern, since ferns used to thrive in the area surrounding the spring. Another opinion is that the name derives from Fruggi or Fruigy—perhaps early landowners.

The water's very low mineral content is the result of its passage through layers of permeable and semipermeable rock. As the water filters through these layers, it loses much of its mineral content.

But the lack of minerals didn't seem to matter much to the A. Manzoni and Company, Inc. of Rome. In 1889 they distributed an advertising flyer which hailed them as Exclusive Distributors of Foreign and National Mineral Waters. And this is what they had to say about Fiuggi; "Always genuine, unaltered, and cool water—beware of imitations—the wholesale trade of all its waters, the true genuine source, gives full warrant of freshness to the public."

It was really in the 1920s and '30s, however, that Fiuggi became the summer resort for the cream of Roman society. It drew, as well, a whole raft of politicians, philosophers, and industrialists.

In 1960, Ente Fiuggi, Inc., took over management of the spa and its waters and moved very quickly to expand the facilities. They did a complete reconstruction and reorganization and built a new bottling plant, which is governed by regulations set down by the Italian Ministry of Health.

In 1970, the spa's treatment centers were completely overhauled. The success of the management of Ente Fiuggi is attested to by the great popularity of both the water and the spa.

Gerolsteiner Sprudel

From Gerolstein, West Germany. This effervescent water is high in calcium and magnesium and is virtually sodium-free. It is lightly bubbled and clean-tasting.

About 300 million years ago, the so-called Devon Sea covered a large part of the European continent. (The sea was formed by an enormous flood that would have made Noah blush with shame.) As the waters evaporated over millions of years, microscopic plants and animals became part of the layers of limestone that were formed. These lime deposits run (in Germany) from Düren in the northeast, to Drier in the south, right through the Eifel Mountains, and right through the area of Gerolstein.

Then, about 20 million years ago, volcanic activity raged through the Eifels and cut through the limestone layers.

scape that owes its character to the volcanoes. What were once threatening, lava-filled craters, for example, are now lovely lakes. Even the company's trademark suggests the water's origin. The lion in the red star conjures a huge mineral spring gushing from the heart of a volcano.

There are actually six mineral springs on the property of the Gerolsteiner company, all of which maintain a consistent year-round temperature and mineral composition. The company employs over 400 people and exports its product to the Common Market countries, the United States, and Canada.

The springs provide the equivalent of one million half-liter bottles daily, which the company uses to produce various products. Aside from the Gerolsteiner Sprudel, an effervescent water, there is also Tafelwasser, a still water; Heilwasser, a

Left, denizens of the Devon Sea; right, the Moselle Valley

One of the results of this was the formation of carbonic acid gas. And another was the formation of huge underground caves in which water flowed and then gathered. The water was enriched by the minerals in the limestone, mingled with the carbonic gas, and was then forced to the surface under great pressure. In fact, when the first well was dug in the area, in 1888, a geyser of water shot over forty meters in the air. Even today, on cold mornings, one can see small clouds of gas rising from fissures in the earth.

The gas in Gerolsteiner Sprudel is removed during the collecting process and then replaced during bottling. This allows for quality control and uniformity of the bubbles.

Gerolstein, "The Town of Wells," is on a tributary of the Moselle River and is situated in land-

slightly effervescent water; and a whole range of soft drinks that use the mineral water as a base. These include lemonade, orangeade, cola, and grapefruit drink.

The reputation of the water in Europe still rests, in part, on its curative properties. It is recommended for ailments of the stomach, liver, gall bladder, intestines, and kidneys.

By 1938, the Gerolsteiner company was among the leading German producers of mineral water. The war, however, destroyed the business totally. It took some time to regroup, but in 1947, 1.5 million bottles were sold. The number rose dramatically to 100 million by 1969, and with the water's current exposure to the American market, the picture for continued growth looks bright.

An effervescent water from Kysibel-Ky-selka, Czechoslovakia (13 kilometers from the world-renowned Carlsbad). The water has a high sodium content and alkalinity, and some say it goes very well with spicy food.

Legend holds that the healing powers of Carlsbad's waters were discovered when a wounded deer was seen jumping into a hot spring

In the western tip of Czechoslovakia is the medieval city of Cheb. And quite close by is a spa that has all-star status among spa aficionados—Carlsbad. Over the years, many notables have been drawn to Carlsbad's oversized baroque splendors, including Wagner, Chopin, Schiller, Beethoven, and even Karl Marx. The waters of Carlsbad are so high in mineral content, by the way, that the merchants are able to offer a unique souvenir for sale. They soak flower blossoms in the water until they become encrusted with mineral crystals.

Karl Marx

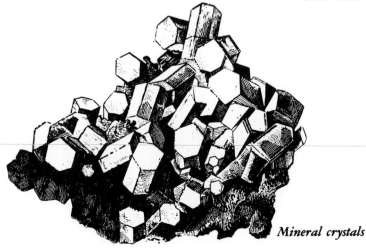

Mineral crystals

The main promenade at Carlsbad

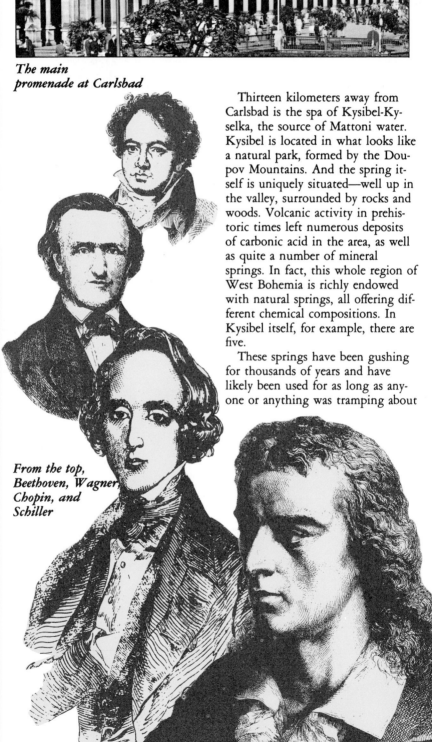

From the top, Beethoven, Wagner, Chopin, and Schiller

Thirteen kilometers away from Carlsbad is the spa of Kysibel-Kyselka, the source of Mattoni water. Kysibel is located in what looks like a natural park, formed by the Doupov Mountains. And the spring itself is uniquely situated—well up in the valley, surrounded by rocks and woods. Volcanic activity in prehistoric times left numerous deposits of carbonic acid in the area, as well as quite a number of mineral springs. In fact, this whole region of West Bohemia is richly endowed with natural springs, all offering different chemical compositions. In Kysibel itself, for example, there are five.

These springs have been gushing for thousands of years and have likely been used for as long as anyone or anything was tramping about the landscape getting thirsty. Archeological finds at various sites attest to this.

These springs were considered a source of spa therapy as far back as the fourteenth and fifteenth centuries. In fact, when Columbus was busily engaged in sailing the ocean blue, West Bohemian spas were already active in water cures.

The history of Mattoni water goes back a year or two itself: to 1522, to be exact, and to a report from one of Carlsbad's most famous physicians, Wenzel Payer de Cubito.

It took five years of work (circa World War I) to industrialize the springs in such a way as to preserve their natural state. And today, there is a modern plant collecting a water that has been bottled and exported for over 200 years.

And it has been called Mattoni all this time. The name derives from the company which first began bottling and distributing the water. During this past century, Mattoni has been exported to sixteen countries.

Mattoni's literature recommends its use for various and sundry ailments (including mixing it with milk for upper-respiratory miseries). But as with all of the mineral waters, don't think of this one as a medicine. And with Mattoni's high sodium content, be especially careful.

The mineral balance of the water remains relatively constant and contains sodium, potassium, lithium, magnesium, and calcium. Its natural bubbles make the water easy to digest as well as an aid to digestion.

Mountain
Valley
Water

®

from
HOT SPRINGS,
ARK. 71901

FAMOUS FOR 100 YEARS

Good for
Everyone

CONTENTS: 64 FL. OZS.
(2 QUARTS)

...CARBONATED

DELICIOUS

...ural water from world-
...mous Mountain Valley
...ring in health-resort area
...f Hot Springs, Arkansas.

Recommended for every-
...g, whenever any water
...y be used.

...licious to taste, at room
...mperature or chilled.

...o recommended for
...king coffee, tea and
...ing, mixing with fruit
...ices, infants' formulae,
...c.

...eral elements, normally
...solution, may be seen
...he sudden temperature
...ge.

Characteristics:

Low Sodium-less than
ten milligrams per 100
grams, or per 8 ounce
glass. (226.6 grams.)

Mildly alkaline - pH 7.8

Uniform analysis, temper-
ature, flow at spring.

Free from urban waste,
pesticides, detergents, never
exposed to open air.

Enjoy 6 to 8 eight ounce
glasses daily, or as your
doctor may direct.

Mountain Valley

Andrew Jackson; right, Hernando de Soto

"The wonderful water from Hot Springs, Arkansas" has a pH of 7.60. It is a still water, mildly alkaline and virtually sodium-free. It has good flavor and character, and won't wear out your taste in daily use.

Hernando de Soto was here in 1541, exploring for gold. He was successful but probably didn't know it. The gold he found was liquid.

The story begins when a band of friendly Indians led the explorer to a region they called Tahmeco, "the place of hot waters." This valley had served for many years as a neutral ground where the Caddo and Quapaw Indians brought their sick and ailing warriors. The diary of the explorer's secretary records that their party rested in the area for three weeks. And de Soto himself wrote that "Indians of many and hostile tribes were at peace, to share the recuperative waters." Many have shared the waters since, because Tahmeco is now what we call Hot Springs, Arkansas.

With that auspicious beginning, it's little wonder that Hot Springs enjoyed a wide and early reputation as a spa. The thermal baths drew people from all parts of the country. In fact, President Andrew Jackson created the Hot Springs reservation in 1832, making it the first (and still only) spa in this country under

Kelso (left) and Secretariat

"Hot Water cooled without, exposure to air, all Radio active gases thus saved."

The Imperial Bath House, Hot Springs, Arkansas

federal administration. It was made a national park in 1921.

The area lies 60 miles southwest of Little Rock, sprawls over 4,500 acres, and contains forty-seven hot mineral springs. But there are also many cold springs as well, and when Peter Greene moved to town in 1870, one of them drew his attention. Lockett Springs it was called, and it had a pretty wide following of its own. So Mr. Greene, a reputable "prescriptionist," bought it and immediately began making improvements. He built a three-story hotel with twenty-six bedrooms, a spacious lobby and parlor area, and an immaculate dining room. He also sent a carriage to meet all arriving trains and transported his guests through the towering pines and oaks that covered the slopes of the Ouachita Mountains. In 1871, he changed the name of the spring to Mountain Valley and started to sell the water locally. And by 1879, it was being shipped to many surrounding states.

It was customary at the time for mineral waters to be used therapeutically, and Mountain Valley joined the parade. An early fan was a Mr. B. M. Feely of New Orleans. His letter was published in the August 29, 1879, edition of the *Hot Springs Illustrated Monthly:* "I came to this

From the left, Nashua, Bold Ruler, and Gallant Fox

place as a last resort five weeks ago, a great sufferer from Dyspepsia for seven years, and could find no permanent relief from the best physicians in our city, and I now consider myself permanently cured."

Of course, there were detractors as well. One of them was the Federal Trade Commission, which rapped the knuckles of an overexuberant distributor who was advertising the water as a cure for almost every dread disease known to humankind.

"World's best water for kidney and bladder troubles."

"Is Radio-Active Mountain Valley Water."

"For Bright's Disease, Indigestion, Diabetes, Arterio-Sclerosis, Gout, Rheumatism, Inflammation of Bladder, Calculus, Arthritis, Sciatica, Neuritis."

Well, creative ad-men will be creative ad-men. The distributor hung his head appropriately, coughed up $500, ceased and desisted, and went along his merry way.

Things moved along pretty briskly during the next years, and in 1879, Greene sold the spring. The Mountain Valley Railroad was built to span the 12 miles from the thermal springs to the increasingly famous cool spring. And just three years later, Mountain Valley received a charter from the state of Arkansas to "ship . . . and sell . . . in all parts of the world." In 1894, Eastern demand for the water was such that the first franchise opened. It was in Philadelphia, and another opened in New Orleans just a short time later. (It is not known if the letter of the dyspeptic Mr. Feely had anything to do with the New Orleans decision.)

Mountain Valley's journey to New York is an interesting tale in itself. The business of America is indeed business.

The story starts in 1908 on a train speeding eastward. Two men had just spent a few relaxing days at the spring and were bound for home. As chance would have it, they decided to eat at about the same time and were seated at adjoining tables in the dining car. Each produced a pint-sized bottle of Mountain Valley

Hearst

to drink with dinner. Not surprisingly, conversation ensued and, after a short time, both agreed it a pity that their friends in New York were being deprived of the water they both found so delicious. They decided, therefore, to form a company that would bring the mountain to Muhammad. The cost was to be shared equally, hands were shook, and, finally, introductions were made. The first gentleman was Richard Canfield, a noted restaurateur of the time and just as noted a gambler. The other man was William Randolph Hearst. And it didn't seem to matter the slightest to either of them that the Hearst papers were doing their damnest at that very moment to put Canfield in jail for alleged gambling operations.

End of story? No. The first carload of Mountain Valley water was shipped to New York with the bottles resting on their sides, like fine wine. But when the train doors were opened, the shipment turned

Left, Marlene Dietrich; right, Kate Smith, official photographer

out to be mostly empty bottles. The chemical composition of the water had caused the old-fashioned corks to disintegrate in transit. New corks brought better luck and New Yorkers have been enjoying the water ever since. Incidentally, Mountain Valley is shipped exclusively in glass bottles. Early trial and error showed that the water picked up unpleasant tastes and smells from any container other than glass, which is chemically inert.

Mountain Valley grew apace. By the time of the first world war, franchises were operating in more than twenty cities, and the number grew steadily after the war. Now there are over 1,000 dealers and distributors throughout the nation. To this day, Mountain Valley remains the oldest bottled-water company in the United States selling water nationally from a single source.

Speaking of a single source, Mountain Valley's is a huge underground reservoir. Water from the surrounding Ouachita Mountains exerts pressure which forces the water up through a bed of marble until it reaches the surface—the Mountain Valley spring. The marble is thought to be 250 to 400 million years old and the spring checks in as a mere youngster of 4,200 to 7,000 years.

Mountain Valley water is consistently uniform because the same quantities of water flow at the same rates of speed through the same rocks. Therefore, the amounts of minerals that dissolve into the water are more or less constant. But the company isn't just settling back and letting Mother Nature handle it all by her lonesome. The company owns almost 500 acres of the surrounding timberland which serves as a preserve for the spring's natural watershed. In addition, the spring has been enclosed to protect the waters from air pollution, and special equipment in the plant's filling rooms treat the air to further protect against contamination. (A comparison of water analyses done thirty years apart seems to show that these protective measures have paid off. The surveys show consistency in the water's make-up.)

Of course, it wasn't all wine and roses during the spa's long and varied history. Take February 19, 1934, for instance, just before noon. Mrs. J. E. Collins, the manager of the Mountain Valley Hotel, saw billows of smoke coming from the attic, so she quickly warned all twenty of the guests and the rest of the staff. Despite everyone's best efforts, in an hour and a half the grand old place was just glowing embers. The closest thing there was to an official photographer of the tragedy was singer Kate Smith, who had arrived the day before, and who was observed busily snapping pictures of the whole affair.

Mountain Valley's list of fans runs the gamut from the Led Zeppelin rock group to Marlene Dietrich. Since 1920, it has been served in the dining rooms of the United States Senate; Anwar Sadat is said to carry it to dinner parties; former president Nixon took it to China on Air Force One; and Dwight Eisenhower announced to a press conference in 1957 that he was drinking it on the advice of his physicians following a heart attack. And it's even possible that the good residents of Little Rock would have been deprived of Carol Channing singing "Hello Dolly" to them if a full supply of Mountain Valley Water hadn't been included in her performance contract.

But not all customers for the water are human. Famous racehorses have trained on it—Gallant Fox, Nashua, Bold Ruler, Secretariat, and Kelso (although every water company seems to claim those last two). And on national television a famous horse trainer told Arthur Godfrey, "Mountain Valley water won't make a good horse out of a bad one, but it makes a good horse a little bit better." *Attention all joggers!* Chew on that one the next time you go to the kitchen tap for a drink.

Carol Channing,
"Hello, Little Rock"

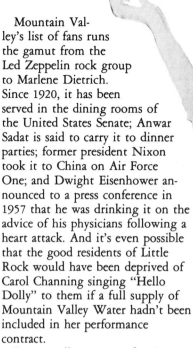

*"The Champagne of Bottled Waters,"
a naturally effervescent water from
Vergeze, France. Light mineral content,
highest in calcium, and virtually sodium-free. The water has snap and
style and may be too bubbly for some,
but it's hard to argue with success.*

People have known about Perrier
for over 2,000 years. Eighty-five gen-
erations have drunk it because they
were thirsty, hung-over, or had indigestion. And then one day, Perrier
became the reigning superstar of
bottled mineral waters. Drink of the
Beautiful People, of show people, of
sports people. So Cartier designed
sterling silver Perrier bottle caps and
openers, a chic clothing store fea-
tured six-packs as window decor,
and a fashionable magazine suggested misting your face with it and
pouring some in your bath to
"make it all tingly."

In the nation's capital, Perrier replaced vodka as the "in" drink. In
Los Angeles, some restaurants
charged the same for *it* as for alcohol. And in New York, Perrier even
helped play the *power game* by be-
coming the status drink, the only
drink drunk by people in the know
(who used to drink a glass of Cha-
blis with a single ice cube).

The Perrier story doesn't begin
with Dr. Perrier, because without
Sir John Harmsworth you'd never
have heard of him. And it doesn't
begin with Hannibal either, although he did get thirsty enough
sometime in 218 B.C. to stop by for
a drink. The Perrier story actually
begins in prehistory, over 140 mil-

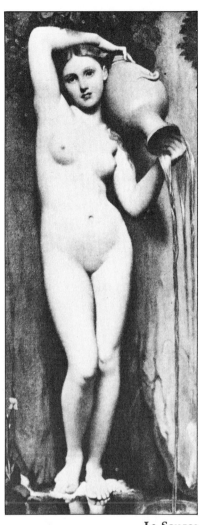

La Source

Volcan

lion years ago. During the violent volcanic activity of the cretaceous period, land masses changed and shifted, faults and fissures developed within the earth, and the gases which account for Perrier's carbonation were released.

The Perrier spring is located on a wide plain in southern France, near Nîmes, in the township of Vergeze. It is bordered by vineyards, with hills to the southeast and wastelands to the north. Over 5,000 meters below the surface of the ground, carbon dioxide gas travels up through cracks in porous limestone. As it rises, it intermingles with clear mineral water, and natural carbonation takes place. From there, the now sparkling water continues to rise to the surface, where it is tapped. Since Perrier is a *single* spring, it is called The Source. (But

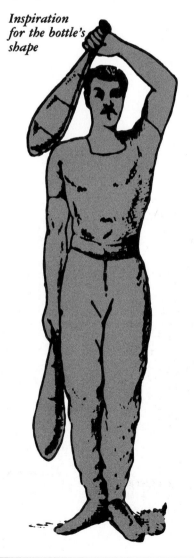

Inspiration for the bottle's shape

the local townspeople, bless them, call it "Les Bouillens," the bubbling waters.)

Today, the gases in Perrier are removed from the water as it comes from the spring and then reinjected as it goes into the bottle. This process is needed to maintain uniformity since temperature fluctuations cause the gas content of the water to change year-round. In addition, a certain amount of carbon dioxide escapes as the water fizzes up from the ground. This has to be put back during the bottling process.

A number of geological factors contributed to the formation of the Perrier spring. Lying beneath it is a deep, mixed layer of white sand and gravel. This mixture acts both as a basin in which the carbonated water collects, and a natural filtration system through which the water passes.

Above the spring is a nonporous clay barrier which stretches for several kilometers in every direction. This effectively prevents any surface waters from seeping in.

The output of Les Bouillens is 21,-000 gallons per hour. But there is no need to hoard. Even the most pessimistic studies show the spring bubbling merrily along for at least another 200 years.

But back to Hannibal. He was thirsty when last heard from, so he rested his troops at Vergeze and drank from the spring. Although there is no record of his reaction to the water, there is also no record of his burning and looting the town. Obviously, Perrier had won over its first Beautiful Person. (It is believed, by the way, that the waters today are virtually identical in mineral content and sparkle to what they were when they tickled Hannibal's fancy.)

Some years later, in the first century A.D., the Romans built baths at the spring. The baths were enjoyed by the legions who were hard at work constructing the aqueduct and the Temple of Diana—both of which still stand about 15 kilometers away in Nîmes.

In the Middle Ages, the spring was left to the townspeople, who bathed in the water and drank it. They called the area the Roman

The Aqueduct near Nîmes, France

Basin and believed the waters to have curative powers.

Napoleon III must have agreed, because in the mid-nineteenth century he granted rights to develop the spring as a source of bottled water. The reason? "For the good of France." (And since that time, interestingly enough, France has continued to keep a paternal eye on the site. By decree, no other wells can be dug within a five-kilometer radius.)

The bottling of the water began various attempts at making the spring into a spa. All attempts failed, however. Yes, even Dr. Perrier failed. But he did succeed in meeting and encouraging a young Englishman to buy the spring. The man was Sir John Harmsworth, whose father owned London's *Daily Mail.* Sir John purchased the spring by selling his stock in the family

Hannibal

business, and decided to name it after the good doctor. Harmsworth also decided to get out of the spa business and into the luxury beverage business. So in 1903, he began marketing on a large scale. He replaced the cabins and hotel with a bottling plant, warehouse, and railroad siding, coined the slogan "The Champagne of Bottled Waters," and modeled the now-famous Perrier bottle after the Indian clubs he used for exercise.

In 1933, the year of his death, 10 million bottles of Perrier were exported all over the world. It could be found in officers' clubs of the British army in India and in almost every fine restaurant and hotel in the United States and England.

After World War II, Harmsworth's heirs sold the company, and today, Perrier employs 1,500 people in Vergeze. The spring itself is no longer visible, however. It lies beneath a huge bottling plant where the waters are brought by pipes directly into bottles.

Sir John Harmsworth

Perrier takes very little getting used to. There is no soapy or salty taste, it's not sour, nor does it remind one of milk of magnesia. In addition, it is among the most bubbly of all the bottled mineral waters.

Some European doctors prescribe the water for such ailments as indigestion and hangover, but the ads in this country simply stress that Perrier has no calories, chemicals, preservatives, flavorings, or additives of any kind and that it is "bottled directly from nature." The company is stressing its use as a soft drink and maintains that 85 percent of Perrier customers use it so. In France, for example, Perrier outsells Coke two to one, and Pepsi seven

The happiness of the short distance runner

66

Tea and Perrier with the British Army in India

to one. Perrier is also confronting the fact that the United States is a nation of sugar-junkies. It offers a recent government survey which shows the average American consuming the equivalent of 295 sugar-laden soft drinks per year. The push is for Perrier as a natural alternative.

Tip: Keep the bottles refrigerated. Pouring it warm over ice will burst the bubbles, and if the ice cubes are made from tap water, they will dilute the Perrier.

$500.00
REWARD

FOR EVIDENCE WHICH SECURES CONVICTION OF ANY PERSON FOR REFILLING
BOTTLES BEARING OUR TRADEMARK, OR FOR SELLING AS POLAND WATER ANY
WATER NOT FROM POLAND SPRING — POLAND SPRING BOTTLING CORPORATION

...bottled just
...om the deep
...Pond water.
...since 1845.

poland®

This untreate
contains
earth mineral
salts or chlor

Mineral Conta...
Total Solids...
Hardness a Ca
Bicarbonates a
Calcium
Calcium as Ca...
Chlorides as C...
Iron as Fe
Iron as Fe₂O₃
Magnesium
Magnesium as
Nitrate - N
Nitrates as N...
Potassium
Silica as SiO...
Sodium
Sulfates as S...
Hydrogen - ...

PURE NATURAL
MINERAL SPRING

WATER

Analysis of
oratory Se...

Poland Water

Calvin Coolidge, left, and Mae West

From Poland Spring, Maine. It comes from the spring as a still water, but is also available with added carbonation in a sparkling form. It has no mineral tang thanks to an almost complete absence of sodium, sulphur, and alkali, and has a full, soft, clean taste as a result.

What say to a multiple-choice test? Four questions. Four points per question. Four minutes to do it. No penalties for guessing. No cheating. Ready . . . begin.

1. This famous rock star insists on having Poland water at all of his concerts and also feeds it to his pet boa constrictor.
   a. Alice Cooper   b. Mae West
   c. Calvin Coolidge d. Gloria Swanson

2. This formidable sexpot is quoted as saying, "I don't drink and I don't smoke; those things tear you down. I'm careful of what I eat, and I only drink Poland water."
   a. Alice Cooper   b. Mae West
   c. Calvin Coolidge d. Gloria Swanson

3. This president of the United States used to write from the White

Alice Cooper with his boa constrictor; right, Gloria Swanson

House and place his order directly with the bottling plant.
a. Alice Cooper   b. Mae West
c. Calvin Coolidge d. Gloria Swanson

4. *This famous actress and classic beauty not only drinks Poland water, but also claims to have bathed in it.*
a. Alice Cooper   b. Mae West
c. Calvin Coolidge d. Gloria Swanson

Answers: 1 a, 2 b, 3 c, 4 d

Perfect score? Good. Sorry there aren't any prizes, but you can console yourself with this tale: In 1800, Joseph, the youngest son of Maine farmer Jabez Ricker, was gravely ill—suffering from what was diagnosed as an untreatable case of kidney stones. Since "last resort" time was fast approaching, the young boy's doctor prescribed regular doses of the water that gushed from a deep granite spring on Jabez's land. After three days, the fever began to break and the doctor's examination revealed that the stones were dissolving. Upon analysis of the water, it was found that the mineral content made for a mild, natural diuretic.

In the early years of the nineteenth century, many similar cures among local residents followed, including the almost miraculous recovery to bursting health of an ox. And not surprisingly, it wasn't long before the Ricker farm was converted into a spa.

The first bottling plant was constructed on the site in 1845, and by the turn of the century, Poland Spring had achieved status as one of the leading health resorts in the United States. As with most spas, it was never clear whether people went there for therapy or socializing. They drank and bathed in the waters all right, but sociability was no less a part of the attraction. The Rickers, however, grew with the spa—from simple farmers to landed gentry. And although the company has changed hands many times in the ensuing years, the Ricker signature still proudly adorns every bottle of Poland Spring water sold today.

One of Poland's advertising lines reads: "It's like having a mountain spring on tap." And this is not solely ad-man jive. The water lacks many of the substances that often leave a mineral aftertaste. It is pure and clean-tasting, and has remained consistently so.

The hotel at Poland Spring

SAPIENTIA DONUM DEI

Poland Spring, Maine Interior of Spring House

Interior of the Spring House

The healthful properties of the water were not isolated until around the 1850s when analyses showed the composition of the minerals present. And the purity and mineral balance of the spring have remained unchanged since the first bottling analysis was done, in 1845.

Some years ago, a slight amount of chlorine was found in the water. After much investigation, the chlorine was traced back to residue left in the bottles from the water used to wash them. From that day forward, the company has sterilized its bottles with filtered water only. And the bottling plant itself uses hospital procedures to guarantee the cleanliness of the entire operation.

One of the major turnarounds for Poland occurred in May of 1977 when the company was purchased by Paul den Haene, a French financier with long experience in the water field. Now, distributorships are growing, and Poland is poised to grab its share of the ever-expanding mineral water pie. Poland is an American product, therefore it has no importing costs and can be competitively priced. It is available in its still form, and also with added carbonation. As the company's PR copy reads: "In truth, it's simply a gentle, refreshing splash from a very old granite spring in Maine. And in a contemporary context, when everything old is new again, what could be more simple or enjoyable."

PERHAPS APOCRYPHAL TALE #3 (Told as the gospel truth at a cocktail party, so judge accordingly.)

One of the owners of Poland Spring over the years was a father of two sons, a confirmed teetotaler, and also a bit of a tyrant.

When the old man finally went to his just deserts, the sons commemorated the occasion by beginning production on Poland Spring Gin, which used the water as its base.

And as if the boys were not satisfied enough with that gesture, the booze was sold in a bottle shaped just like dear old dad.

Ramlösa

From Helsingborg, Sweden. A sparkling water to which small amounts of carbon dioxide are added during bottling. It has gentle bubbles, light alkalinity, and an appealing flavor.

Next time you are invited for dinner at the king's house in either Sweden or Denmark, don't be surprised at the bottles of Ramlösa you see on the table. . . . No, that's not quite royal enough. . . . Next time you are invited for dinner at the king's house in either Sweden or Denmark, the water poured into your cut crystal chalice from a finely worked decanter by a white-gloved servant will be Ramlösa. By a special warrant, this mildly carbonated mineral water is served regularly at both these royal courts.

The Ramlösa spring is located in the southwest part of the city of Helsingborg, which is on Sweden's southeast coast. In fact, it is very near the southern tip of the country, separated by only a few miles of water from Copenhagen. The spring itself sits in the middle of a beautiful park, surrounded by old beech, oak, and chestnut trees.

The geological history of Ramlösa is not known, but the existence of the spring has been since the late 1600s. It was started as a health spa by Johan Jacob Döbelius, a physician from Germany, on June 17, 1707. Dr. Döbelius was later appointed professor of Medicine at the nearby University of Lund and ever since then, the professorship has been combined with the title of

King Karl XIV Johan of Sweden

head physician of Ramlösa (this is possible since the university is closed for the three months in the summer that the spa is open). It is, by the way, the visage of Dr. Döbelius that stares out at you from the label of the bottle.

The spa was originally frequented by nobility, but as the years passed, strictures relaxed and the clientele broadened. A frequent early guest of the spa, though, was Queen Désirée, once a "fiancée" of Napoleon Bonaparte. After parting from Napoleon, Désirée married one of his most famous generals, Jean Baptiste Bernadotte, who was later appointed king of Sweden under the royal name Karl XIV Johan. King Johan, it should be noted, was the first ancestor of the still-ruling Swedish royal family.

Ramlösa functioned as a health spa until 1975. It offered comfort-able accommodations, gentle service, and beautiful gardens and walkways. There was even a "philosophic passage," if you suddenly felt the need to get your head together. One businessman who attended a seminar at the spa was heard to remark, "In this atmosphere, it is impossible not to get good ideas."

The curative properties attributed to the waters during the spa days were mainly for liver, kidney, and gall bladder miseries, but today, Ramlösa is marketed throughout Scandinavia and the world for its taste and varied uses.

The spring was originally owned by a private company, AB Ramlösa Hälsobrunn, but since 1975 it has been part of a very large Swedish conglomerate.

The Ramlösa spring is located 200 feet below ground and is free from environmental pollution of any kind. The average output is about 75,000 gallons per day and there seems to be no end in sight to the spring's active life. The new Ramlösa bottling plant was completed in 1973 with a capacity of 65,000 eleven-ounce bottles an hour. Small amounts of carbon dioxide are added during bottling, which account for Ramlösa's slight carbonation. In terms of mineral content, however, the water is undoctored—what nature gives is what you gets.

The International Society of Gastronomes, Chaine des Rôtisseurs, proposes three commandments: no smoking between courses (huzzah!), no speeches while eating (huzzah! huzzah!), and mineral water should be served with wine. Ramlösa's slight carbonation and lightness of taste make it a good choice for all apprentice gastronomes. Also try it between courses. It is a good palate cleanser that can help you savor what's come and appreciate more fully what's on the way. It can also be used with good results as a mixer, as an accompaniment to sweet liqueurs and cognac, and also with chocolate and other heavily sweet desserts.

Queen Désirée

The Italian Alps

From Bergamo, Italy. This water is slightly alkaline, with a pH of 7.29, and has a clean taste. It's high in calcium, magnesium, chlorine, and sodium and has added carbonation to make it sparkle.

According to Italian historians, San Pellegrino water has been known and used since the twelfth century. And records show that Leonardo da Vinci traveled to the spring from time to time when the Sforza family of Milan acted as his patrons in the early sixteenth century.

The commercialization of the water also started in Milan, with the formation of the San Pellegrino Company in 1899. The company was formed to distribute the mineral water of the San Pellegrino Spa, which is located in Bergamo in the Italian Alps. The spa is still open and functions from late spring until the fall chill intrudes in early October.

Although the company was started to distribute the mineral water only, today it markets a selection of soft drinks that use the water as a base. In fact, the company sells so many bottles in one year that if you put them end to end, they would reach one-third the distance to the moon. (That's one of those really great statistics that prompts as many questions as the bottles they put end to end. Who thought it up? How? Why? Was there a bonus involved? *Exactly* one-third the distance to the moon? Just how many bottles *is* that? Was the figure arrived at longhand? By new math? By pocket calculator? Etc., etc.)

San Pellegrino is exported to five continents and is known in over fifty countries. The company's bottling facility is huge—about 120,000 square feet—and quality control is stringent. Sometimes as many as 400 samples of the water are taken daily for analysis.

The prime reason for the water's purity and consistency is the area's natural filtration system. The water flows upward through layer after layer of limestone, sand, and porous volcanic materials.

The water's added carbonation yields small bubbles, making San Pellegrino a good mixer for wine and liquor, and just as effective straight with a wedge of lemon or lime.

Saratoga Vichy

*From Saratoga Springs, New York.
"The King of Table Waters" is
strongly alkaline, has aggressive bubbles, and is rich in sodium, calcium,
magnesium, and potassium. The water
is recarbonated, but since July 1978, the
taste is just as it comes from the earth.
(Before that date, additives were included to maintain the water's familiar
flavor. So if you tried it before and
didn't like it, give it another shot.)*

George Washington

Beneath the area of Saratoga
Springs lies what remains of a prehistoric ocean, embedded in limestone. Many minerals are contained
in the layers of porous rock—potassium, iron, calcium, magnesium,
and sodium. Water is forced up
through these layers by natural carbonic gas and is enriched along its
journey by the minerals there. The
water moves upward from about
180 feet and travels through some
150 feet of rock to a convenient
geologic fault which yields the
spring.

The Indians of the Saratoga area
thought highly enough of the
spring to call it "the gift of the
Great Spirit," and highly enough of
the water to bring around Sir William Johnson. Sir William was a
British colonial leader in America
who entered the fur trade and acquired great power among the Indians of the Mohawk Valley. He
soon joined the Indians in spreading
the word about the therapeutic
values of the water, leading George
Washington, among others, to become an early enthusiast.

A gazebo in Saratoga

The springs are located in upper
New York State, about 30 miles
north of Albany. The spa itself is a
few miles south of town, in a 1,500-
acre state park. It offers magnificent
swimming pools, golf, horseracing,
four big bathhouses, and a first-rate
performing arts center. And perhaps
what it offers most of all are re-
minders of a glittering past that
many would like to revive.

The spa emulated its European
counterparts of the early nineteenth
century, and the latter part of that
century was Saratoga Springs's fa-
bled age. The Beautiful People of
the era flocked there for the casino
gambling, the elegant hotels, and
the horseracing.

Sir William Johnson

Diamond Jim Brady

Miz Lillian

In 1833, the number of vacationers to Saratoga jumped from 6,000 to 8,000. A green stamp give-away? An all-you-can-eat-for-a-nickel buffet? No. Someone figured out how to propel railroad cars by steam instead of horses. At first, the cars cranked along at a blistering 15 miles per hour, but a few observers had a notion that the contraption might eventually go a wee bit faster.

Among the cast of characters that Saratoga could call its own was Diamond Jim Brady. Diamond Jim was worth about twelve million dollars, and the fact that he was crude and almost illiterate didn't seem to stop him from making deals with the other railroad men who frequented the spa. Probably the best thing about him, though, was that his constant companion was the beauteous Lillian Russell. Strollers delighted at the sight of Miss Russell pedaling through Saratoga's boulevards on a gold-plated bicycle, a small token of affection from Diamond Jim.

Saratoga's first racetrack was built in 1863 by an ex-heavyweight boxing champ, John Morrissey. Morrissey was fine at organizing projects, but not so fine with world happenings. He announced his first program of four days' racing only to discover that all the available horses had been requisitioned for the Civil War. But John persevered and managed to locate enough horses to make his races a great success. (If all this is true, one's heart goes out to the poor, retired plowhorses recruited for the race who found

themselves trying to remember how to gallop while being urged on by a screaming crowd.)

Another Saratoga regular was Bet-a-Million Gates. Gates was a turn-of-the-century high roller who needed no urging whatsoever. He would bet fortunes at the track for two and three days at a crack. Story goes that Bet-a-Million won so much money one day that he had to carry it all home in an enormous shopping basket.

And Saratoga also drew "The Prince of Gamblers," Richard Canfield (the same Richard Canfield who went into partnership with William Randolph Hearst on a Mountain Valley Water franchise). Well, seems that Canfield opened his casino in the summer of 1894 and was the first gambling entrepreneur to allow his customers liberal credit instead of requiring cash on the barrelhead. Carrying large sums of money on one's person, he felt, ruined the line of one's evening clothes.

Saratoga, however, was in the water business as well as the spa business. And the company's advertising in the early 1900s trumpeted the therapeutic values of the water:

The Most Delicious, the Most Refreshing, the Most Efficient of All NATURE'S REMEDIES. Assures Sound Digestion! Sound Sleep! And Sound General Health.

The water was recommended for indigestion, for diseases of the kidney and bladder, for insomnia ("Drink freely, say two or three glasses before retiring"), and as a tonic ("Use the water frequently through the day in moderate quantities. This will tone up the system, imparting increased vigor to all the vital organs"). And all this at a bargain price. Around 1907, $12.00 would buy 100 pints and $8.50 would fetch 50 quarts.

The claims made by the company today are a trifle different. Here's some recent advertising copy from Saratoga Vichy which touts the benefits of the water with tongue firmly planted where it should be—in cheek.

The Joys of Saratoga Vichy Straight

1. *Helps Food Taste Better.* Aficionados claim Saratoga Vichy cleanses the palate—enhancing the taste of everything you eat. There are no published studies of this, however. Only word of mouth.

2. *It Helps You Watch Your Weight.* Saratoga Vichy is nature's own sparkling diet drink—with *no* calories. Great news for thirsty people with slim hopes.

3. *A Cure for Hangover?* So some people claim. It has also been rumored that consumed the night before, Saratoga Vichy ameliorates the effects of mornings after. As temperate Yankees with unshakeable principles of moderation, we'd have no first-hand proof of either hypothesis.

Above, a Saratoga jet; below, the Saratoga jet set

Spa Reine

The Casino at Spa

Montaigne, visited in 1580

From Liège, Belgium. A still water with low mineral content, a pH of 5.75, and almost no sodium. Light, smooth, and soft to the taste. The motto of the spa is "The Future Cannot Be Understood Except in Light of the Past."

The town of Spa lies 32 miles from Liège in southeast Belgium, very near the German border. The name of the town derives from the Latin *espa* (meaning fountain) and it was quite well-known as early as the first century A.D.

Pliny the Elder, in his *Natural History,* mentions that the waters of Spa were "already famous." And if you're not comfortable with an ancient Roman naturalist as a source of information, there is even more tangible proof. In 1851, when one of the bath sites was being restored, Roman coins were found bearing the likeness of Emperor Nerva, who ruled in the first century.

Spa was only a small town of a few hundred people in the sixteenth century, but it was able to boast of being a meeting place of nobility. Under the rule of the bishop princes of Liège, the town enjoyed widespread acclaim and popularity. For example, Henry VIII's personal physician, Venetian Augostino,

Roman Emperor Nerva

Austrian Emperor
Joseph II started
a tradition

Victor Hugo

spoke up on behalf of the waters. In 1565, Thomas Gresham (whose famous law states that "bad money drives out good") was quite grumpy indeed at "having lost the commodity for going to Spa this year." And Montaigne mentioned Spa in his famous *Essays* and visited there in 1580.

It was in the sixteenth century that doctors began to study the therapeutic qualities of the water. Those who valued its properties looked for ways to administer it to patients who could not travel to Spa. In addition, many people who visited the town wanted to be able to continue the "cure" in their own homes. Two needs yielded one solution: Export. Thus began the commercial exploitation of the waters of Spa.

In the very beginning, the water was shipped in small brown bottles that were carefully stacked in straw baskets and carried by porter to Liège. From there, the water reached its final destination by either land or sea. Export documents for the year 1632 show that almost 100,000 bottles were exported in this manner.

The late seventeenth century, however, heard some grumbling in the small village. Complaints were registered with the ruling bishop prince that all the commerce was causing undue congestion, without the townspeople deriving any financial benefit from it.

The Right of the Seal was therefore established. It was actually an export tax on each bottle of water shipped from Spa. One third of the tax went to the church, a third to the tax controller, and the last third reverted to the town. The date was January 27, 1688, and the Right of the Seal actually marked the day that export became the town's principal economic activity.

Spa grew markedly throughout the eighteenth century and soon became known as "The Queen of the Towns of Waters." Facilities were expanded and new ones built. Before the 1730s, the bath facilities were rather crude and the accommodations catch-as-catch-can. But in 1734 the first hotel was built, and in 1773 a major treatment facility was constructed—with four hot baths, one cold one, an open-air pool for swimming, a steam bath, and a shower. This actually ushered in Spa's greatest era of popularity—the eighteenth and nineteenth centuries.

Inscribed in the town's "Golden Book" were the names of emperors and kings, as well as the nobility of science, art, and music. The eighteenth century records visits by the queen of Belgium, Peter the Great, and Leopold II of Belgium. In 1781, Austria's Emperor Joseph II visited and is said to have begun a tradition that is still honored today. Joseph discovered it best to drink the water and then assist its journey through his body by a bit of a walk and some light conversation.

The eighteenth century also brought more scientific inquiry into the properties of the water. Treatises of the time called it "light" and "very subtle" and suggested that the baths were good for the heart and overall circulation.

The nineteenth century saw Spa in full flower with visits by the shah of Persia, the composer Offenbach, the Duke of Wellington, Czar Nicholas, Victor Hugo, Disraeli, and Dumas.

Europe's high society convened in Spa starting in the beginning of June, and spent the entire summer there. This prompted another of Spa's nicknames, "The Café of Europe."

In 1860, a new facility was built in the center of town to meet "modern requirements and hygienic demands." It is this building, expanded and further modernized over the years, that still houses Spa's thermal baths.

Exploitation on a grand scale actually began in 1869 when Emile

Grand Hotel Britannique, German Army headquarters, 1918

Dhainaut plunked down 2.5 million gold francs to turn Spa into a first-class resort and water exporter. But all-too-soon thereafter came World War I. Spa served as the headquarters for the German army in 1918, and just two years later, it again played a major role in world affairs. It hosted the Spa Conference in which Germany presented its plan for war reparations to the Allied forces.

Today, Spa is still quite active, retaining much of its air of grandeur in its hotels, parks, walkways, and casino. Its physical setting is lovely, as the surrounding forest comes right to the edge of town. And it has added the allure of golf, tennis, riding, and auto and motorcycle racing to its theater and concert programs.

NATURAL ALKALINE MINERAL

VICHY

VICHY · ETAT

CFV CFV

FRANCE

Compagnie Fermière de Vichy — Vichy (All

CELESTINS

CONVEGO S Ltd - ELMSFORD - N

(1 ST. 1

Vichy Célestins

From Vichy, France, the seat of the Vichy government in 1940, and the home of vichyssoise soup. The water is salty, slightly effervescent, and high in potassium and calcium. Although some say it has a "volcanic tang" that takes some getting used to, it is one of the most popular waters in the world.

At the time of the Roman conquest, Vichy was known as *Vicus Calidus,* "the hot town." And the old "hot town" was also an ancient "hot spot," because 2,000 years ago Julius Caesar turned the place into a rather luxurious resort. Vichy was chock-a-block with temples and also with bathing pavilions where the Romans could take the waters at their leisure. In the old part of the city, numerous ruins and artifacts have been found that attest to the extensive construction that once existed there.

But Attila the Hun and the rest of his friends were never known for refinement in their aesthetic sense. They swept down from the north in waves and destroyed the city. The springs then fell into disuse and were all but forgotten.

Toward the end of the fourteenth century, however, Louis II, the Duke of Bourbon, found the region charming and decided to install himself in Vichy. So he restored the springs, built a castle, and surrounded the town with imposing walls. In 1410, Louis founded the Convent of the Célestins, and under his protection the city prospered and the people felt secure. However, a successful attempt to oust the Bourbon kings ensued, and on February 7, 1576, the Prince of Condé entered the city, which did not defend itself. The next twenty years saw Vichy as the unfortunate centerpiece in a tug-of-war. Attacks and repulses, intrigues and threats prevailed. Finally, in 1590, the city was taken by the Marquis d'Urphé.

The marquis burned the city to the ground, pulled down its towers, churches, and walls, and massacred the people. Unfortunately, this tragedy was not the end of Vichy's travails. The city was taken once more, after a war between the Catholics and Protestants.

It took the patronage of Louis

Atilla the Hun in a quieter moment

Madame de Sévigné

Napoleon Bonaparte

XIV to bring stability back to Vichy. In 1636, for example, the first thermal station since Roman times was built. The area prospered under Louis and became so important that later, Napoleon Bonaparte personally dedicated the spot where the springs are now located.

But the real fame of Vichy actually came in the charming personage of Madame de Sévigné. It seems that she spent two seasons at the spa and wrote about it so wonderfully that it became known at court. Soon, everyone wanted to go.

Madame de Sévigné was a most engaging woman—gay and lively, with a bubbling sense of humor and keen intellect. All of her published letters are addressed to her daughter, but they were widely read and helped make Vichy *the* place to be.

The good woman, it seems, suffered from rheumatism, which was the prime reason for her first journey in 1676. And although virtuous in almost every way, Madame de Sévigné was known to overindulge occasionally in good food. After extended bouts of this, she would drag herself to Vichy for a water cure (the seventeenth-century version of a stint at a fat farm). Her first departure for Vichy was marked by an elegant little dinner party for her friends. The menu? Pigeon tart.

Madame de Sévigné couldn't abide the doctors at Vichy. She found them overbearing and unbearable, and said so. She also had a word or two to say about the flavor of the water. She remarked that it tasted of saltpeter and was strongly disagreeable!

There were no casinos at Vichy then, nor were there theaters, concerts, or game rooms. The nobility who visited led more simple lives than visitors do today and mainly sought out each other's company for diversion. It seems that many people were cured at Vichy just by being in the company of Madame de Sévigné, whose vibrant personality worked wonders with those suffering from depression or compulsive eating.

She tells of a typical day's sched-

The Grand Casino at Vichy

Julius Caesar

this little underground place and there one finds a tube with hot water that a woman aims at different parts of her body. It is a very humiliating thing.

It may very well have been so, but Madame de Sévigné endured nobly and contributed greatly to making Vichy "The Queen of Watering Places."

Vichy is in the Auvergne Mountains, in the valley of the Limagne. Prehistoric volcanic activity caused abundant boiling springs to form in the area, springs that provoked fear in the ancient inhabitants, who thought them either magically or divinely inspired.

But it wasn't magic—it was geology. The springs come from immense underground lakes, so huge that their size has never been measured. The waters are heated by great masses of granite that come into contact with heat from the earth's core. This heat also releases hydrogen which begins to make its way to the surface. As it does so it passes over rocks and unites there with available oxygen. Presto . . . water, and the lakes are constantly renewed.

ule which finds everyone up at 6:00 A.M. and down to the fountain for a drink (she remarks that everyone looks awful). They stay at the fountain until 12:00, then it's lunch at someone's home, an afternoon walk, and cards. A light meal highlights the evening, and then it's to bed by ten. This was the schedule that Madame de Sévigné virtuously followed, hating every minute of it.

Part of the cure was showering in the waters, but the showers at the time were far from refined. Madame de Sévigné writes about them, too.

I started the shower this morning and it is a great rehearsal for purgatory. One is completely nude in

Still propelled by gases within the earth, the water rushes upward and charges itself with all the minerals it meets. Through layer upon layer it moves, until it emerges. This process has gone on for thousands of years, and the resulting water remains consistent in quality, temperature, and mineral composition.

The springs at Vichy are found in a protected area of some 37,000 acres. They are owned and operated by the French government. In fact, Vichy has been said to epitomize the spas of France.

Tens of thousands come each year from March through September. Many come to cure various ail-

Ad from The New Yorker, *February 1929*

Louis II, the Duke of Bourbon

ments, and heaven knows there's enough information on the subject. On file in the Vichy library alone are no less than 489 scientific works on the water. There are four sources in the spa and each is recommended in various ways for ailments of the liver and stomach, allergies, nutritional problems, and children's diseases. And even the 1915 index of the Army Surgeon General of the *United States* listed 28 monographs and 92 papers on Vichy's water.

But aside from the cure-seekers, many come for a restful vacation (although you'd never know it from looking at the seemingly endless parade of distractions offered by the spa—Vichy has even hosted the world's water-skiing championships and, for those who like them, cattle shows, too).

Ancient bronze figures unearthed in the area represent "patients" holding drinking cups, further evidence of the spa's long tradition of water cures. Today, the water that is bottled and exported to over ninety-two countries comes from the cold spring of Vichy, Célestins, named after the convent established by Louis II. Célestins has a lower mineral content than the waters of the three hot springs.

Louis XIV

The River Allier at Vichy

A still water from Vittel, France. The water is high in calcium, and magnesium, low in sodium, and has a pH of 7.05.

The town of Vittel is in the Vosges Mountains, in the heart of western Europe, five hours from Paris by train. It is a centralized access point to the major cities of Belgium, Switzerland, Germany, Italy, and, of course, France.

The region in which Vittel is located has been inhabited for thousands of years. Archeological evidence, in fact, shows the presence of people since the neolithic age.

kilometers away at Grand are the remains of what must have been a sumptuous "pleasure palace." Grand was the center for worship of the god Grannus. After the Romans consulted their oracles and physicians in Vittel, they would undergo various purification ceremonies and then go to the temple. They would sleep there and awaken the next morning with what they called "peace of mind." No doubt the climate and geography of the region added to the sense of relaxation, as it still does to this day.

The formal history of the waters begins with a lawyer from the town

The pool at Vittel

Relics have been found throughout the slopes of the surrounding mountains—fragments of pottery and other evidence of the tribes who were active there long before the Romans came on the scene.

The name Vittel is not Roman, as is sometimes assumed. It is more likely derived from *Weg-Thal,* or the "path through the valley"—the name given to the area by the Lotharingian tribe, people who came in search of the "resting place of the warrior." The name was changed by the Romans much later and, after many transformations, it finally became Vittel.

The Roman presence, however, is very much in evidence throughout the valley. Fragments of statues have been found, as have coins and even the remains of stoves used by the Romans to heat the water.

But it was not only the water that attracted the Romans. A few

of Rodez, Louis Bouloumié. The revolution of 1848 found Monsieur Bouloumié on the "wrong side" as the commander of the Republican Guard, and the coup d'état of 1851 found him making a quick trip to Barcelona for his health. Although the trip might have saved him from a meeting with the guillotine, he became quite ill in Spain. A special dispensation allowed him back into France, where he tried to cure himself at a renowned spa. He tried twice and failed both times. Then a friend told him of an unexploited spring nearby that gushed out of a farmer's field. The spring was called the Fountain of Gérémoy. Having little to lose at this point, Bouloumié went there and drank the water. He was cured. But since he had some trouble believing in miracles, he decided to have a chemical analysis made. The analysis was done and revealed the virtues of the spring. So in 1854, Bouloumié

Louis Bouloumie

One of the first Vittel bottles

bought the spring and all of the farmer's land for 3,950 gold francs.

At that time, the town of Vittel had 1,300 inhabitants. The springs themselves were virtually neglected except by the people of the village. Those seeking spa cures went to nearby Contrexéville.

In 1856, Louis Bouloumié built a structure that contained a small number of rooms and showers. Six people ventured to the spa that year for a cure. In 1860, ten times as many came, and Bouloumié decided that maybe he had the makings of a good thing. So he decided to do it up right. He built a hotel, a restaurant, a casino—and Vittel's reputation began to spread.

In 1863, the Grand Hotel opened its doors. It was a showplace. The sisters of the convent of Saint-Dominique embroidered the linen, a famous Parisian designer made all the furniture out of sycamore and mahogany, the silver came from the renowned Christofle, and two famous chefs from Paris arrived to rule the kitchen.

Three years later the Beautiful People started to come, the royalty of France, and the rest of Europe. One of the spa's earliest aficionados was Lord Marlboro, reputed to be an ancestor of Winston Churchill. The Lord, so the story goes, liked to take his water mixed with a liberal measure of good whiskey.

Bouloumié died in 1869, but the spa and the city continued to prosper. The Vittel springs remained in the hands of the founder's family, and even today, the president of the company is an ancestor.

If a time traveler returned to Vittel today, much would seem the same, The decor and surroundings have remained relatively untouched (one does not even see cars). Although the city now has 7,000 inhabitants, twenty-five hotels, and many restaurants, the area has retained its calm and serenity. Over 6,000 people per year travel to Vittel for rest and cures. Louis would be proud.

Ah, the French. They have a saying in the area: "To go for a cure at Vittel does not signify that one has to ignore the pleasures of the good flesh." This inevitably leads one to rhapsodies about the food of the region—blue trout with almonds, fruit tarts, river shrimp, and the local honey that must be made by very, very contented bees.

Going under the presumption that what is good for your insides must also be good for your outsides, Vittel water is packaged in elegant spray cans with a very fine mist. Fashionable ladies keep the Vittel in their refrigerators, and spritz themselves for refreshment on a hot day.

In 1972, the municipality built a sports complex. The facility is so impressive that it was chosen as a preparation site for the Olympics. In 1977, 8,500 athletes from around the world gathered there for training sessions. And if *you've* a mind to visit, there's even a Club Med in the area.

There are actually three major springs in Vittel, each with different mineral content. The geological formations of the area are such that

the water springs from very deep underground sources. They are totally protected against pollution of any kind, and their flow and mineral content remain constant.

The first bottling plant was built in 1912, nine years after the French Academy of Medicine recognized the waters and declared them to be of "public interest." The modern facility now in operation is hidden away, so as not to spoil the serenity of the area.

From an early Vittel poster